I Can't Live
Like This
Anymore!

Lilada Gee

Live Fully!

Lilada B. Gee
608-217-8281 M
608-257-2453 x225
lilada@lilada.com

Hayah Publishing House
Madison, Wisconsin

Hayah Publishing House
655 West Badger Road
Madison, Wisconsin 53713

Cover and book design by
Kris Grauvogl • Greybird Designs
www.greybirdesigns.com

ISBN 0-9774549-0-8

Printed in the United States of America

Dedication

This book is lovingly dedicated to my children, Alexandra and Christian. Every day you give me a reason to live, love and laugh. And to God, every day you give me the strength to do so.

Appreciations

To my fabulous and incredible big brother Alexander Gee, Jr. Thank you for affirming, inspiring and loving me unconditionally, every single day of my life. You always told me that I could fly; even when I was too afraid to crawl. I've got my wings now...watch me soar!

To my dazzling sisters from another mother: Desiree Fleming, my best friend, and Denise Maddox, my muse. You have been an incredible source of strength and support to me during the writing of this book. You encouraged me to keep going long after I wanted to stop. You both help me to see who I really am!

To my many amazing girlfriends who read, laughed and cried along with me as I labored on this book. Thank you for rallying around me with your words of enthusiasm and editorial feedback.

And finally to my mother; for releasing me to write this book with truth and candor.

Table of Contents

Contents

For years, my sister Lilada struggled with clinical and post-partum depression, an anxiety disorder, low self-esteem and even insomnia! The weight of her story and the pressure of her childhood secrets were simply overwhelming. She confided in me that she needed to "get this crap out." Meaning, she had to free herself, her soul, her children and other victims by breaking all the unwritten rules and telling our family's darkest secrets. I cringe and celebrate at the same time.

Lilada's candor, humor and audacity make this book an extremely poignant and captivating read. Her inviting style is so colorfully vivid that I forgot that I was reading about my own family. She is a quintessential storyteller!

I recently found an entry in one of my old journals from March 2nd, 1995, about my sister …

"When you break a bone, therapy is often required in order to regain use or mobility. I think Lilada is moving into a season of healing and God is teaching her how to walk, how to live, how to trust, how to receive, how to love and be loved and how to appreciate and be appreciated. It's a form of "love" therapy. Although many patients never regain full health or proper usage of injured areas…Lilada will! Sometimes recovery is more painful than the initial trauma because the injury only happened once, but the pain of recovery is like reliving the injury over and over again. If Lilada endures the therapy, she will "walk and live" again.

This book is part of her therapy—and I believe it is a part of each reader's therapy as well. The message of this book is going to revolutionize the lives of countless men and women by giving them the strength to break their silence, to betray their secrets and confront the lies and liars in their lives. Nothing is as freeing as the truth—and this book will give readers permission and courage to embrace the truth of their lives.

If Lilada could've found a book like this as a struggling young woman, perhaps her healing wouldn't have taken so long. Thank goodness you don't have to wait…let the healing begin!

Alexander Gee, Jr.

It was no accident that you picked up this book. Your destiny drew you. I have shed blood, sweat, and tears over this work. In the end, I gave it to God, and I asked Him to place it into the hands of every woman who needs to hear what I have to say.

When I first began to write this book, my motivation was completely altruistic. I thought that the writing was for you, the reader, to help to free you from a life that God never intended for you to live. And it is. But I have discovered along the way that the writing of this book was first for me.

I had a need to write my story. Although the pull to do so was strong, it did not make the process any easier to endure. I struggled to find the correct voice. I want it to reach many women, like myself, who have lived desperate lives full of pain and sorrow. My deepest desire is to offer my testimony of encouragement to them so they too can overcome and be victorious. I want my book to touch the hearts of mothers, to help them to be in tune with their children: aware of what is going on in their lives through observation, open communication, and other means. I hope that mothers who have endured awful circumstances will read this book and become conscious of their deep need for healing so that they can raise whole children who don't have to pay for sins they did not commit.

This is why I am writing this book: for me, my children, and those whose pain has been disregarded. I have learned that pain will not be ignored. If we do not face it on a conscious level, it does its devastation on an unconscious level. Deep below the surface a raging river was flowing through my inner self destroying everything good that was left inside of me. It's now time for me

11

to face it. I hope that as I share my painful story of victory, you, too, will be able to turn your face to your pain, acknowledge it, deal with it, and overcome it.

My very soul was sick unto death. I searched to and fro seeking a healing for the disease of my soul. When all my hope and strength were gone, all I could do was grab hold of the hem of the robe of Jesus Christ. It turns out that that was enough to bring the deliverance I had sought for so very long.

The writing of this book has taken me on a journey that for many years I was afraid to take. I lived devoid of deep feelings and emotional connections. I could not afford to feel, for feeling what I was going through, when I was going through it, would have destroyed me. When I began revisiting those painful experiences, I encountered post-traumatic stress. Can I just be myself and be honest here? The truth is it hurt like hell! It felt like I was reliving each devastating experience of my life, only this time it was in 3-D and living color. Everything that I did not feel the first time, I felt. I wanted to, once again, hide from the pain behind a façade, but the mask no longer fit.

When I first began writing this book, I tried extremely hard to be religiously correct. I used nice language, and I was careful not to say anything that would offend anyone in my past or my present. The pages of this book were full of facts and figures, but they weren't full of me. I put the book down for an entire year. For an entire year I convinced myself that I was finished. For an entire year I refused to touch it. After a year, I heard it calling out to me.

I was afraid to pick it up again. I wasn't sure if I could face the truth that was written on these pages. I wasn't sure if I could ask myself to go any deeper than I had gone already. Within me, I knew that for this work to be true, I had to reveal my truest self: the good, the bad, and the ugly. So, I went through again: word by word, line by line, page by page, and I inserted my heart and my soul.

This book tells the story of my life in a very honest, no-holds-barred manner. I have used real language that at times is, let's say, spicy. But this is me, pure unadulterated me. This book isn't sweet. It isn't nice. But it is powerful! And in these pages lie the secrets to the deliverance of your soul.

Chapter One
Things Aren't Always As They Seem

I can't live like this anymore! I can't, I can't do it!
I sat totally alone in the darkness of my room and in
the darkness of my life. It was closing in on me, and I
couldn't escape it. A feeling of doom consumed me.

The streetlight in front of my house glared through
my window casting distorted shadows. I looked from
one end of the room to the other. There was not one
single clear place on the bed, shelves or floor; my
belongings were scattered across every surface.
Walking though my room was hazardous.

I buried my face deeply in my hands as bitter, salty
tears poured from my eyes and dripped through my
fingers making tiny, rhythmic taps as they hit my bed.
My chest ached from the desperate weeping that had
begun as a few tears and had now become a hysteri-
cal cry—a cry for my life.

My closet was filled with elegant formalwear: silk
skirts, silk blouses, silk dresses, fancy Sunday-go-to-
meeting hats, Coach, Prada, and Louis Vuitton purses,
and a leather skirt that I could barely squeeze one
thigh into. Clothes too big, clothes too small, clothes
that I was never going to wear again this side of glory;

many with store tags still hanging from their sleeves filled my closet, spilled out onto the floor, wandered across my room, and lay across my bed.

Gadgets and gizmos that faxed, e-mailed, called, recorded, added, subtracted, and translated from Spanish to English were scattered across the floor and piled up on the dresser and shelves. Half-filled journals-some with only one or two pages of writing-notebooks and scraps of paper filled with my deep thoughts, brilliant ideas, and revelations from God littered the floor of my room like bits of tickertape carelessly left after the New Year's Eve celebration in Times Square. Trash.

The stench of dirty dishes, sitting in the kitchen sink, stained with last week's meals filled the lower level of my house. My kids' little feet would get stuck on the kitchen floor, which was covered with their accumulated spills. The living room was chaotic too, cluttered with self-help books, several versions of the Bible, backpacks, children's dirty clothes, children's washed clothes, that needed to be put away, art projects, toys, stinky little socks, and yes, more paper. (I owe a few trees an apology.) I won't even begin to talk about the basement. There aren't enough pages in this book to begin to describe the abundant, miscellaneous mess that was down there.

The shit that cluttered every square foot of my house called out to me, every day. There was so much of it, all demanding attention at the same time. It was too much and it was too loud. I couldn't decipher what it was saying. It was trying to give me a message, one that I wasn't ready to receive, so I tried to drown it out with more shit to fill up all of the places that were still empty. That's all I knew to do.

I hated every second of every minute of every hour of every day of the way I was living, but I refused to accept how out of control that my life was, to even be able to begin the process of stopping my life's madness. My external environment, albeit out of control, really wasn't my basic maladjustment. It was a mere reflection of the hellish life that I was living within. It wasn't all the shit that surrounded me that was killing me; it was all of the shit inside me.

I surrendered, willing to accept the fact that I had to do it, I just didn't know when or how. The sooner the better, I thought. Visions of my past raced through my head, cruelly taunting me. Every painful memory reminded me, encouraged me, cheered me on to just do it.

I unclenched my eyes, now bloodshot and swollen from my fierce crying, I looked at my wrists. What would it feel like? I wondered. All I have to do is slide the blade across my wrists, cut, cut, and it'll all be over. I slipped into an almost hypnotic state as I envisioned myself slowly, almost lovingly, slitting my wrists with a sharp razor releasing myself from prolonged misery. I pictured the warm, red blood rushing out of my veins, running down my body like a snake slithering across hot sands, creating an oasis of my blood on my lush purple carpeting. Drip. Drip. Drip.

I have been a Christian for the past thirty-some years, and at this point of my life, I felt as if I didn't know who God was and He didn't know me.

Why am I living this agonizing life? My God, don't you see me, don't you care? I have served you since I was a child. Is this the best you can do for me? Why, God? Why have I had to endure so much pain? What did I do to deserve this? This is not how my life was supposed to be.

Every day I would wake up and put on one of my sharp coordinated outfits with matching designer bag and shoes. Until I had added a few sprays of my favorite scent, White Linen by Estée Lauder, I wasn't completely dressed. Stepping over piles of clutter, confusion and chaos, I would put on my fake "everything is right with my world" smile and walk out the door to face the day. According to all outward appearances, I had the perfect life.

Sister, let me tell you, I had it made. I mean I truly had it going on! My life was just as I had imagined it would be—no, better. Ask anyone who knew me: they will tell you that I had the perfect life. If they are truly honest, they may even tell you that they envied me. I know what they thought. They thought I had everything a woman needed and everything a woman wanted. And they were right. Don't get me wrong, I'm not boasting. I thanked God each and every morning when I woke up and each and every night before I went to sleep for all my many, many blessings.

Do you want to know just how good I had it? I was married to my college sweetheart, Duane. He looked like Stedman—no, Will Smith in Bad Boys. He was the type of fine that caused women to stop, look and appreciate. He was a tall drink of water: nice physique with caramel brown skin and good hair. He was a pretty boy, just what I liked. Not only did he look good, but more importantly, he was saved, sanctified, filled, and baptized with the Holy Ghost, and that with fire. He was the man of my dreams, and he was mine. All mine.

We had a beautiful daughter together, Alexandra. Really, I mean my baby girl was absolutely breathtaking. She had soft curly black hair and big brown eyes that would melt ice even on the coldest of days. She was my dream darling, and her favorite place in the whole world was in my arms. She was sweet, loving, and a bundle of joy. Not only did I have my little princess, but my belly was swelling with a new baby on the way. I could hardly wait to love and kiss on my new baby.

My husband adored the ground that Alexandra crawled on. He loved to spend time playing with her, rocking her to sleep in his arms or filling her belly with laughter by throwing her up in the air. She was his pride and joy, and he too joyfully anticipated the arrival of the new baby. What a terrific dad, huh?

My family and I had a great place to live. Our home was in a quiet eastside Madison neighborhood, only minutes away from my favorite frozen custard joint, Michael's. It was a great older home, my favorite kind. We had a two-level apartment with gleaming hardwood floors, beautiful woodwork throughout, glass-paneled doors, and antique glass doorknobs. We had all of those wonderful amenities and unbelievably low rent. Sounds a little like paradise, doesn't it? I had an ideal job and a fabulous boss, who just happened to be my big brother, Alexander, whom I adored. We had worked with his wife, Jackie, and our mother to build a successful nonprofit social service organization that serves children, youth and families, from the ground up. I had the opportunity to work alongside my family in a field I was passionate about and get paid. Couldn't ask for much more than that now, could I?

I had a very supportive family. Through thick and thin, I could count on my family to be right by my side whenever I needed them. My mother and stepfather had raised me. They had been together since I could remember. Growing up I had never gotten to know my biological father, but it didn't bother me too much, because I had my stepfather and he was always there for me. Everyone always said how lucky Alex, my mother and I were to have him in our lives. He was the dad we'd never had. He treated us as if we were his flesh and bone. He paid for my lavish wedding, he was at the birth of my first child like any proud grandfather would be, and if I ever needed anything, I mean anything, he would always provide. I was really blessed to have him in my life, wasn't I?

He and my mother had gone through some tough times earlier in their marriage, when I was around eleven years old, but they had been able to work through it, put it behind them, and rekindle their love for one another. My brother and I were able to see a great example of how a married couple could overcome even the most difficult of challenges and stay together.

After many years, when I was twenty-five, not long after I had gotten married, they finally decided to call it quits for good. Even after my mother and stepfather were divorced, he was still intimately involved in our lives. He and my mother maintained a good relationship. The two of them even work together now. If you saw them together, you would be surprised to know that they were divorced from each other. That's remarkable, isn't it?

My mother and I enjoyed an extremely close relationship. Wherever you saw one of us, you'd see the other. We spent most of our free time together, laughing, talking, shopping, and eating out at Cracker Barrel and Red Lobster. She visited my husband and me frequently at our little paradise. It was really good always to have her around to give her insightful opinions and suggestions. She offered many helpful hints on how to have a good marriage. Don't you think every mother and daughter should have such a wonderful relationship?

⁂

Now, my sister, you have had a close-up look at my life. I am sure you can understand what I told you earlier. I had it made, right? I had a fantastic life with nothing in the world to complain about. Those around me admired all that I had and were intoxicated by my life.

Well, I hate to have to tell you, but I've decided to walk away from it all—person by person, thing by thing, place by place. I know what you are thinking right now. You are thinking that I must be some kind of crazy fool. You want to know why in the world I would walk away from a life that was so wonderful, don't you? But things aren't always as they seem, are they?

Like Mother, Like Daughter

Like mother, like daughter, the paths we take
Impact the decisions that our daughters will make

They watch what we do,
More than they listen to what we say

They're taking mental notes,
Preparing for what they'll do one day

Generational curses can be stopped
dead in their tracks,

If we, as mothers, would change how we live,
what we say, how we act

If you're not careful, my sister,
Of the things that you say and you do,

You will look in the mirror one day and see,
That your mother has become you.

19

Swack! The midwife hits her little yellow behind. The baby begins to cry. "It's a girl!" the midwife enthusiastically tells my grandmother. She raises her up high so that the new mother can catch her first glimpse of her daughter. Her view of the baby is still obstructed, though: she is crying too. Not tears of joy. She is crying bitter tears of sorrow, for she is ill prepared for the little one's arrival. Verline is the wrong thing at the wrong time.

The midwife cleans her up and places her in the reluctant arms of her mother.

My mother was at risk from the moment she was born.

My mother was later to learn that she was the product of a scandalous relationship my grandmother had with a married man. The news of this affair traveled fast in their small Missouri town. My mother believes that the shame and ridicule my grandmother suffered from this caused her to have a difficult time bonding with her. She always felt that her mother loved her other children more than she loved her.

Mama—as my grandmother was called—had been raising two children alone with no husband in sight. By this time she had already lost two other children to illness. She had nothing going for her, and everything against her. She was poor, uneducated, black, and a woman living in the South during the height of discrimination and segregation.

She had gone from man to man, looking for something that she lacked, but could not find. She stayed with one until the thrill was gone and it was time to move on to the next. By the time Mama met my grandfather, Homer Grays, she was emotionally spent from all the heartbreak and disappointment.

I used to ask Mama about her relationship with my grandfather. I loved to hear about her life. She told me that she and Homer spent a lot of time laughing, talking, and playing cards. He was a breath of fresh air in a very stifled life. They began as friends. Their friendship progressed, and they became lovers.

When Mama found out that she was pregnant with my mother, it was an occasion of regret rather than celebration. When she told my great-grandmother Ada that she was pregnant, again, her response was *"It's a shame for you keep having all of those babies and you're not married."*

My grandfather found out that he was going to be a father from rumors circulating in the small country town of Hayti, Missouri. At first he denied that he was the father, I think that his wife insisted that he did. There were no DNA tests around back then, but he had been there. My mother's beginning was less than planned, anticipated, and welcomed. What a way to enter the world!

Ready or not, when November 11, 1939, rolled around, my mother was on her way. She was born Verline Shaw in her mother's bedroom. My grandmother had celebrated her twentieth birthday less than a month before. Verline was the fifth child born to my grandmother, the second child born to my grandfather, who, by the way, was nowhere around on that day or many days, weeks, months, and years afterward. It would be years before she would even know who he was.

Growing up without her father was really devastating! I believe that the absence of Verline's father from her life set the tone for everything that followed for her from day one. Remember, your father is intended to be your number-one protector. When he's not there, you must make your way through life without the protection and leadership that God intended. Here is what happens to the life of a girl who is raised without her daddy.

Mama met Louis Conroy Benjamin Franklin Evans (we kids affectionately called him Papoo) through his sister, Sane. She had recently ended a long term on again, off again relationship with Alec Cooper. Two children were born in this union, my aunt Ada and my uncle Wilbur, who died as an infant. Mama described Papoo as a very nice man, a gentleman. She says he was good to her, and good with her kids.

Most importantly, Papoo rescued Mama from a life of shame as the young woman with all of those bastard kids. He redeemed her. He legitimized her. He was just what she needed, right when she needed it. They married, and eventually my youngest aunt Bessie was born of their union.

Verline must have just turned five when Papoo moved in. Shortly after Papoo and Mama had been married, my grandmother contracted tuberculosis (TB). Back in those days TB was almost always a death sentence, but the grace of God spared my grandmother's life. Papoo kept the kids while she recovered. Mama was impressed that he stayed by her side during a very difficult time. She appreciated the support he gave her.

By all accounts, my grandmother had hit the jackpot! She was on track for living a destitute life, trying to raise her children on her own. She had found a man who was committed to loving and providing for her and to fathering her four fatherless children. Mama trusted him without hesitation. He was a hard worker and a good provider. He brought his paycheck home every week and took care of things around the house; he didn't run the streets, and he never raised his hand to my grandmother.

Everyone thought Papoo was the greatest. He was nice, likable, and fun to be around. He was never one to stir up any trouble. He was helpful, dependable, and reliable, an overall great person—well, that is unless he was drunk. When he was drunk, he was an abusive tyrant. Everyone had hell to pay when he was three-quarters through a cheap bottle of wine.

Truly Papoo was the only father figure my mother and her brothers and sister ever really knew. Mama insisted that all the kids change their last name to Evans, his last name, to honor all that he had done for them. Plus, it added to Mama's legitimization process to have all her kids bear the same last name. They all thought the best of him. Turns out they really didn't know him at all.

To outsiders, they seemed the perfect family. Times were hard, working as share croppers, but they had nearly everything they really needed. What people did not know was that life inside their "perfect" little family was a living hell.

I don't know when Mama and Papoo's relationship began to go sour, but it did. I suppose they had the ups and downs of most couples, but after a while, it seemed there were more downs than ups.

Verline adored Papoo, though she knew he was not her biological father. She used to wish he were her real father. She was his shadow. Everywhere he went, my mother was right behind him. She loved and trusted him like a daughter. He used to show her extraordinary attention, the attention that my mother so desperately craved from her mother. She once shared with me that she and Papoo used to spend a lot of time together. She would be his companion at night clubs; yeah, I know, what the hell was my grandmother thinking, right? She also told me that he would buy her special things that he wouldn't for the other kids.

When she was six, Papoo began sexually abusing her. He abused her from age six until age thirteen, when she finally got up the courage to tell her mother what had been going on.

Mama believed her. She embraced her. She protected her. Verline openly wept in her arms, the desperate tears she had suppressed for seven long and damaging years. They wept together. Verline exhaled a sigh of relief. She had a great sense of freedom and safety. It was finally over, and now she could go on to live a life free of sin and shame, free of guilt, free of abuse. Free!

Before Verline had the chance to get used to her newfound peace and safety, though, without warning things began to change. Mama announced to her that Papoo would continue to live with the family. Verline felt as if she had just been pushed out of an airplane without a parachute. She knew that she was going to hit the ground and be shattered.

The day that my grandmother decided Papoo could continue to live in the house with their family, Verline lost all sense of self. If she had any self-worth left, she lost it on that ill-fated day. She would never again feel safe in her world. She had no place to call home. She retreated to her room, which became her hiding place.

Mama wasn't willing to deal with whatever shit she thought the cost of leaving Papoo would bring her. Was she afraid of what she thought people would say? Was she terrified of trying to make it on her own now with five children? Could she not bear the thought of once again being an unmarried woman with all of those bastard children? Whatever the reason, she decided not to deal with it; so instead, she passed her shit on to my mother to deal with.

My mother was perplexed, bewildered, disturbed, saddened, disappointed, furious, terrified. She felt as if she didn't really exist. She could not understand this at all. She could in no way conceive how her mother could even begin to consider staying with this sick pervert of a "man." What was he doing in their lives, in their home, back in her mother's bed?

Surely it should have been enough for Mama to know that a grown man, who happened to be her husband, had put his man-sized dick into her daughter's virgin vagina. You would think finding out that he had been abusing Verline for seven years right under her nose would have been enough. What would it take—Verline wondered—for her mother to rescue her? Love her? What else could she conclude but that she didn't matter, that she didn't have worth?

Daddy?

Daddy? I've never used that word with anyone I knew
Daddy? I never had one, what was I supposed to do?

Daddy? Why weren't you around to look out for me?
Daddy? Without you there to guide me, how could I see?

25

Daddy? You never wiped a tear, and I cried countless
Daddy? If you were present, my life would not
have been such a mess

Daddy? Didn't you know that I need you?

Daddy?

Swack! The doctor hits my little brown behind. I begin to cry. "It's a girl!", he enthusiastically tells my mother. I take in my first breaths of air and begin to cry. He raises me up high so she can catch her first clear glimpse of me. Her view of me is still obstructed, though: her eyes are filled with tears. She is crying, just as I am. Not tears of joy at the birth of her new baby. She is crying bitter tears of sorrow, for she is ill prepared for my arrival. A nurse cleaned me up and placed me in my mother's reluctant arms. I am the wrong thing at the wrong time.

I was at risk from the moment I was born.

"Come over here and give me some sugar, little girl." I look at the man smiling at me; I hesitate to oblige his request. I don't want to kiss him or hug him or anything else him. I don't know him.

"Go on," my mother urges me, giving me a shove; I mean a gentle push in my back. *"Give him a kiss."* Why? I think. I thought kisses were for Mommy, Mama and Aunt Ada. I wasn't used to kissing a man, especially one that I didn't have the slightest idea of who in the world he was. I still hesitate, even though my mother has given me the green light. I'm only three years old; to me every stranger is a danger.

We are at his beauty salon on the south side of Chicago, and he is pressing a big-breasted, wide-hipped, nosey woman's hair. She is trying her best to figure out what is going on between us all, and so am I. I could feel her eyes and the eyes of the other stylists and everyone else who was getting their hair done all looking at me, trying to see what I was going to do. *"Reach into the cooler and get out any soda that you want,"* he tells me from across the room as he continues to pull the hot comb through his client's nappy hair.

I didn't even have to think twice about following those instructions. I was so excited to get my soda that I almost fell over into the chest. Hey, when you're three, it doesn't take a whole lot to excite you. I choose a grape soda, yummy, my favorite. It tastes so good to me. It's cold and it's sweet as it bubbles down my throat. *"Hey, maybe this guy isn't so bad after all,"* I say to myself; I take a few more swallows of my grape soda to muster up the courage that I need to make my way over to this stranger and allow him a quick peck on my cheek. I figured that was the least that I could do for that delicious grape soda.

I let him have his kiss, but then I run as fast as my little legs will take me, returning to the safety of my mother's lap and continue to drink my soda. Umm, it was good to the last drop.

When I think back over that visit, there was something about that man that resonated within me on an intuitive level. I say this because growing up, I can remember loving Curtis Mayfield and Martin Luther King, both of whom resembled my father, only my father was without the fame and regrettably, without the fortune.

❧

My mother and my grandmother had had a tumultuous relationship. Desperate to find an escape from her family's chaos and just as desperate to find love, at nineteen, my mother, Verline, married a man she thought would provide both. Alexander Gee was her prince charming.

But soon after my mother said "I do," her handsome prince turned into a wart-infested toad. Her fantasy faded to black as the reality of her fairytale proved to be a nightmare. Her days were filled with beatings, and her nights were filled with vain apologies, promises to never do it again, and pledges of undying love. She stayed with Alexander through the black eyes, bruised body, the massive cut on her arm (she still bears the scar some forty years later), his accusations that she was cheating—the truth being that he was—and all the other drama in between. Why? I don't know. Maybe she found it just a little bit better than home. Maybe it reminded her of home.

For five long years, my mother lived at the end of Alexander's fist. She stayed until after the birth of my older brother, Alexander Gee, Jr.

One day little Alex, no more than a year old, attacked his dad to protect my mother during one of their fights. This was the clincher that made her leave. She decided that she didn't want her son growing up hating his father, so she gathered her strength, her things and her baby, and left. Funny thing is, he ended up hating his dad anyway.

By the time my mother met Sam Payton, she was emotionally spent from the fierce relationship that she had endured for far too long. She was depressed and disappointed by her failed marriage. She felt that she needed something or someone to rescue her. Sam was a breath of fresh air in a very stifled life. My mother tells me that she and Sam spent a lot of time laughing, talking, and listening to country music, of all things. Their relationship began as friends; their friendship progressed, and they became lovers. That was until...

When my mother found out that she was pregnant with me, there were no hip-hip-hoorays, congratulatory baby showers, or registering at the local Sears and Roebuck. It was a time of "what in the world have I done?", "it can't be!" and "how am I going to tell my mother," rather than of celebration. She was a single mother, still scarred emotionally and physically from her broken marriage. Struggling to make ends meet with one child, now she was going to have two.

During this distressed time in her life, she turned to my grandmother. For support? I guess. For love and understanding, I'm sure. She found neither. My grandmother's response to her was *"You mean to tell me you laid your naked behind up there and got pregnant?"* (I guess if she'd had her clothes on, it would have been okay, huh?)

This is where I must admit that I get confused by some Christian folks. My grandmother was a licensed missionary in the Church of God in Christ. She was a powerful woman of God, a prayer warrior. She knew demons by their first names and could cast each and every one of them out with one, "Loose here!" Not to mention the fact that as my mother's mother, she should've been the first one to offer compassion, considering that she herself had had eight children by five different fathers, only one of whom she was married to. She of all people knew what it felt like to be in my mother's situation. It would appear to me that this would have been a fantastic ministry opportunity to demonstrate the mercy of God. I don't know, but it seems she should have been a bit more sympathetic, don't you think?

Well, my mother didn't get the support she so badly needed from her mother, but surely she could depend on her friend and lover to be by her side, right?

My father discovered that he was going to be a new daddy from a phone call he received from an overworked and underpaid caseworker at the local Cook County welfare office. My mother had applied for welfare to support her growing family, but in order to get her benefits, she had to name the proud new father-to-be.

The caseworker was short, direct and to the point, as she had a huge stack of additional calls to make to other unsuspecting and unwilling fathers. He denied that he was the father. Men! I don't understand why they act so surprised when a woman that they are fully aware they had unprotected sex with becomes pregnant. It's like they forget how this whole process works.

I was born on December 17th, 1965. My mother named me Lilada Bess Gee, after my grandmother, Lillian and my mother's two sisters, Ada and Bessie. I was the second child born to my mother and the third child born to my father, who, by the way, was no where around on that day or for many days, weeks, months and years after.

My dad was in no way, shape, form, or fashion ever there for me. Other than the grape soda incident, I don't remember ever seeing my father again until I was a teenager. My mother never even talked to me about him. I think I was about eight when I discovered that I was a "Gee" in name only. When my mother, Alex, and I would go visit our Gee aunts and uncles, they always treated me and Alex the same, but I knew that there was a difference in the way that Alex, Sr. treated me. He'd hug Alex, he'd hug me, but he would hold Alex on his lap and kiss on him. He'd give Alex money, he'd give me money, but he'd always give Alex more. In my little mind, I just thought moms and dads liked boys better. Little did I know.

I found out, by a mishap, that Sam was my father. My mother overheard me answering someone who asked me who my dad was; I said Alexander Gee, Sr. She later pulled me to the side to tell me the rest of the story. She told me that she thought that I always knew Alex Sr. wasn't my dad. Well, how would I know if no one had ever told me this information? My last name was Gee just like my brother's, we'd all go visit the Gee family, my mother never talked about me having a different father, I didn't have a clue. Don't get me wrong, it's not as if Alex Sr. was a father to me or my brother, but at least I knew who he was and I knew his family as my own.

Even after this conversation with my mother, it wasn't until I was twelve years old that I knew who Sam was. I started asking questions about him as I got older. I wanted to know who he was and why he wasn't who he should be to me. He sent me a photo of himself. It was the first time that I had ever seen him and known him as my dad. I studied that picture over and over again. I looked just like that man. I used to look in the mirror at myself and I would see a reflection that I didn't fully recognize. I saw a lot of my mother in my face. But that smile, that's not her smile. I finally found my smile when I looked at him. I had his face and I had his smile, but what I didn't have was him.

Growing up without my father was really devastating! His absence in my life made me needy and vulnerable, defenseless and exposed; longing for something that I deserved to have and required, but never received. I felt little, unimportant, disposed of, and insignificant. There is a good reason that God designed it to take two to make a baby; all props to all the wonderful single mothers out there, but one sure as hell cannot completely and sufficiently do the job meant for two. No matter how magnificent a job we single mothers do in raising our children or how well they turn out, there is still a deep longing in the heart and soul of every child for what God ordained.

The absence of my father from my life helped to set the stage for everything that followed for me from day one. Am I saying that my life would have been perfect if my father had been there? No, I don't foolishly believe that. But the worst of my life would have been better if he had been. He was supposed to be my number—one protector and giver of unconditional love, guidance, identity. He wasn't there to give me any of that. I had to make my way through life without the protection, leadership and love that God intended for a father to give his child. Growing up I felt that if I wasn't good enough for the love of my father, then who was I good enough for?

I have since asked him a dozen of a dozen of times why he made the decision to opt out of my life. There has never been an answer that he's attempted to give that could satisfy my question. I have never and will never understood how my father (or any father of any child, for that matter), could know that I was his child and still make the freewill choice not to be a part of my life.

Sam fathered a total of eight children. Two of them were older than me, the rest younger. Yes, he was a busy, busy man. He sounds like a deadbeat dad, doesn't he? The ironic thing is that he knows how to be a father. You know there are some men who just don't have a clue. You wouldn't want to leave a baboon in their care. Not Sam. He was and he has always been there for his other seven children, those older than me and those younger than me. He's loved them, protected them, shared his wisdom, smiled as the proud daddy in the audience at their games and performances, encouraged them, and supported them. He's fathered them. To them he's Daddy. To me he's just Sam, a man I barely know.

I don't know where he was born. I don't know who his parents were. I've never met them. I don't even know what they look like. They knew that I existed, but never cared to meet me. I don't know how many sisters and brothers he has. A lot, I know, but I'm not sure of how many. I don't know the name of his best friend, whether or not he prefers baseball over football or basketball over tennis. I don't know if he likes his steak rare, medium or well. Coke or Pepsi. I don't know who his role models were growing up. I don't know Sam Payton. He's my father and I don't even know him.

My father? Humph! He never changed my diaper, fed me a bottle or rocked me to sleep at night. He never paid one red cent in child support. He never bought me a pair of shoes, a pair of pants, a shirt, cute little lace-trimmed panties, or a warm coat to protect me from the harsh Midwest winters.

He never chased any boogie-men from under my bed. He never kissed me on my forehead and tucked me in at night. He never comforted when I was scared, telling me that he would protect me from anything and anyone.

My father was never at a single birthday party to tell me to make a wish as I blew out the candles. He was never at the Christmas tree smiling as I opened up the special present that he had picked out for his little girl because he knew that it was what I really wanted. He never ever gave me a Christmas present. He never kissed a boo-boo when I fell and hurt myself, telling me that it would be all right. He never wiped a tear away from my eyes.

He wasn't there to walk me to the bus on my first day of school. He never looked at one of my report cards or congratulated me when I did well or encouraged me that I could do it, when I didn't. He never met any of my teachers, or attended a parent-teacher conference. He never quizzed me on my times tables.

He never threw me up in the air and caught me. He never carried me on his shoulders so that I could feel like a princess on her throne. He never tickled me and made me laugh until I almost wet myself. He never danced with me standing on his shoes.

He never took me to the zoo to see all of the animals, and tell me a little something about every one. He never took me out for a cone of my favorite ice cream on a hot summer's day. He never held on to the back of my bicycle, helping me to balance it until I could ride all on my own. He never took me to the candy store or gave me a quarter to buy all the penny candy I could eat.

He never attended one of my grade school violin recitals.

He never met any of my friends, drove us to the mall and slipped me a $20 bill and said *"Don't tell your mother, 'cause you know you didn't wash the dishes."* He never told me to stay away from the wrong crowds. He never told me to "just say no" to drugs. He never told me about the birds and the bees and how not to get stung. He never met a boyfriend or scared the living daylights out of him, threatening what he would do to him if he ever mistreated me.

My father never told me that I was beautiful, special, loveable, unique, talented, smart, funny, creative, or worthy, or that I was anything at all.

He never. He never, because he was never around. Here is what happens to the life of a little girl whose Daddy never. . .

Chapter Four
Everything Is Going To Be Alright

All Is Well

All is well, don't cry anymore,
Everything is going to be alright!

The past is behind you, your knight is here,
Your future looks so bright!

All your cares he will ease,
You will have all the things you've wished you had

He's all the man you've desired,
And to your two little kids he'll be a dad

All of your dreams are about to come true,
Just when you believed they were going to die

He's all that you need, just when you need it,
Sit back, take a breath and sigh…

Lilada Gee

The beautiful fairy tale that my mother had imagined didn't quite work out the way she had hoped it would with her first love, Alexander. Her relationship with Sam didn't evolve into a life-long love affair as she had desired. She continued to long for finding the love of her life, her true soul mate. Just when she was ready to give up hope...

My mother met george fleming jr. through his sister, Pearl. She lived downstairs from us when we lived in an apartment on North Hamlin.

My mother tells me that when she first met george, he was interested in her but she didn't have the same interest in him. He was several years younger than she was. She wasn't looking for a boy; she needed a man, a real man in her life. She needed a man who would be able to help her bear the load she had been carrying all by herself, with not just one, but two descendants of deadbeat dads.

My mother thought that george had some good qualities so she set to unite him with my aunt, her younger sister Ada. She threw a surprise birthday party for Ada and invited george—in hopes of getting him off of her trail and hooking the two of them up. When the party was over, the food put away, and the guests gone, he stayed.

george was a simple country man new to the city from Clarksdale, Mississippi. His classroom had been the cotton fields, where he and his parents, sisters, and brothers (twelve in all) worked long, hot days to make just enough to linger below the poverty line. He couldn't read or write, but he knew the value of a hard day's work.

george was just what my mother needed when she needed it. He would go out of his way to help her. He would give her money to pay the bills, always offer to carry her groceries upstairs, and help her fix things around the apartment. He was a well-mannered, perfect gentleman. Yes, my mother tells me, he was good to her but most importantly he really seemed to care for Alex and me. He was like an ice cold glass of water on a hot summer's day; he refreshed her dry, thirsty soul.

Our families became close. My mother's youngest sister, Bessie, met the Fleming family through us. She and Jerry, george's younger brother, eventually married and had six children. So the Flemings were family.

I had just turned two when george moved in with us. Not long after, our family faced a major tragedy. The doctors diagnosed my mother with cancer. She had to have surgery to remove her uterus. As far as children were concerned, Alex and I were going to be it for her. While she was in the hospital, george showed my mother that he was just the man she thought he was. He took care of Alex and I, he even did my hair-well, sort of.

I remember going with him and Alex to the hospital to visit my mother. She was so impressed that he was standing by her side during a very difficult time. Though she wasn't yet ready to allow herself to love him, she appreciated the support he gave her. His actions during her time of need confirmed that she had made the right choice in welcoming this man into our lives. Turns out he was just what we all needed, just when we needed it. In our crisis, george rose to the occasion and proved that he was more than just a sweet young thang in love with my mother: he was a man, a man whom she could depend on. That was something she'd never had. She exhaled.

When I was four years old, one of my mother's longtime girlfriends moved her family from Chicago to Madison, Wisconsin, so she could attend the University of Wisconsin as a returning adult student. My mother, a highly intelligent woman, was a factory worker in Chicago. She went from one dead-end job to other, earning just enough to make ends meet.

Our neighborhood in Chicago was starting to get really bad. An older boy threatened to rape me. I didn't even know what rape was, but from the way my mother reacted when I told her, I knew it was bad. She decided moving to Madison would be an opportunity to give us a better life. Not only could she go to college to make herself more marketable, she could provide a safer environment in which to raise Alex and me.

We moved to Madison in July 1970. Madison was the land flowing with milk and honey. It was simply beautiful. We had never seen so much water in our lives. We could leave the doors to our house and car unlocked, and no one would break in to them and steal from us. We could leave our bicycles out in the yard and wake up the next morning to find them lying just where we'd left them. It was like living in another world, and we loved it. Just one thing was wrong: george hadn't come with us. He didn't want to leave Chicago.

It wasn't long before he missed his newfound family, though, and decided to join us in Madison. We were glad, because we had all missed him too; he was able to find gainful employment and began to enjoy Madison almost as much as we did.

My mother and george were the king and queen of house parties in Madison. They painted our basement pink with psychedelic accent colors, hung beads at the door, and burned incense. It seemed there was a house party every weekend. Keeping in line with the seventies, there was music by Al Green and Marvin Gaye, card playing, drinking, fried chicken, and reefer at every party. Folks we knew and folks we didn't know would stream through our front door and make a beeline to the basement. Alex and I would sneak out of our beds at night to spy on the adults' goings-on. We saw some crazy stuff. We thought they were some crazy fools.

My mother and george were able to make a good life for us in Madison. We lived in a fantastic neighborhood, just blocks from the lakes, parks and fishing. We had good friends and we lived in a safe environment. Life was good, and it seemed like it could not get any better.

By all accounts my mother had hit pay dirt! Sister, let me tell you, my mother had it made, I mean she truly had it going on! Finally, her life was just as she had imagined it would be-no, better. Ask anyone who knew her: they will tell you that she had the perfect life. If they are truly honest, they might even tell you that they envied her. I know what they thought. They thought that she had everything a woman needed and everything a woman wanted. And they were right.

I Can't Live Like This Anymore!

She was the envy of all of her friends. Every one of her girlfriends wanted themselves a "george." Let me tell you about how good she had it. She had found a man who was committed to loving and providing for her and fathering her two fatherless children. He was a hard worker and a good provider. He brought his paycheck home every payday, took care of things around the house; he didn't run the streets and he never raised his hand to her. My mother was used to love hurting, but this didn't hurt at all. My mother trusted him completely.

george was the greatest. He was the real deal. He was kind, caring, likable, and fun to be around. He was never one to stir up trouble, and if any did start, he was quick to try to bring peace or leave. He was helpful, dependable and reliable, an overall good man.

He even won over my grandmother, by no means an easy woman to please. She thought he was the best thing since sliced bread. Whenever our mother was out of earshot, Mama used to tell Alex and me that our biological fathers never did and never would do anything for us. She told us that george was more of a father than they had been or would ever care to be. She insisted that we should change our name to Fleming, to honor all george had done for us. I'm not quite sure how she thought we, at ages five and seven, were going to accomplish the name change thing, but she put in her two cents anyway.

Me? Oh, I adored george. As far as I was concerned, things were working out for all of us. Not only did my mother get a man, I got a daddy! I used to secretly wish that he were my real father. It really didn't matter, though; my love for him couldn't have been any stronger. I was his shadow. Everywhere he went, I was right behind. I felt the love and trust for him that only a daughter could have for her father. Like a starving child opening a Red Cross care package, I found everything I needed and had been longing for. I was satisfied. He gave me the love and attention I had been yearning for all of my life. george did all that things for me that my father never had. I want you to fully understand: to me this man wasn't my mother's live-in boyfriend, he was my daddy!

It was george who made sure that we had a place to live and food to eat. It was george who bought me shoes, clothes, and gave my mother the money to buy me the cute little flower lace-trimmed panties. It was george who made sure every season that I had a warm coat to protect me from the harsh Midwest winters.

It was george who was there to chase away any boogie-men from under my bed and kiss me on my forehead and tuck me in at night. It was george who comforted me when I was scared, telling me that he would protect me from anything and anyone.

It was george who was at my birthday parties to tell me to make a wish, as I blew out the candles. It was george who was at the Christmas tree smiling as I opened up the special present that he picked out for his little girl because he knew that it was what I really wanted. It was george who kissed my boo-boos when I fell and hurt myself, telling me that it would be all right. It was george who wiped away tears from my eyes when I cried.

It was george who threw me up in the air and caught me and carried me on his shoulders so that I could feel like a princess on her throne. It was george who tickled me and made me laugh until I almost wet myself.

It was george who proudly sat next to my mother at my grade school violin recitals. He knew my friends, drove us to the mall and slipped me $20 bills and said "Don't tell your mother." He was there to tell me to stay away from the wrong crowds and "just say no" to drugs.

It was george who was there to tell me that I was beautiful, special, loveable, unique, talented, smart, funny, creative, worthy. And it was george who was there to teach me about the birds and the bees...

I can't sleep. For days, for weeks, I toss and turn every single night, like a ship being hurled to and fro by the wind and the waves in an angry sea. I wake with my heart beating outside of my chest and my mind racing so fast I cannot keep up with the thoughts.

The dreams are happening again. I can't make them stop. I jump out of my bed and I pace back and forth, back and forth, trying to find peace some damn where.

Thoughts that my kids may be in harm's way bombard my mind. My heart beats faster. I rush into the bedroom to check in on Alexandra and Christian to make sure that they are okay. They are safely asleep in their beds. They look so cute when they're asleep. I steal a kiss from Christian's juicy cheeks. I steal another kiss from Alexandra's pretty little face. I stare at her after I kiss her. She looks so small, so innocent. She's only six years old; she's still just a baby. I didn't know that six was so little...

Terror pounces on my back and sinks its toxic fangs into my neck. Its cruel venom paralyzes me at a time and in a place that I have tried my whole life to *escape. I am caught in the middle of a flashback. I'm six again, and I am feeling all of the degradation, damnation, disintegration, deterioration, dilapidation, and desecration that my body, mind and spirit were kind enough to spare me the first time. I am consumed by fear, anxiety, anger, depression, hate. I am so afraid; I wish my Grandmamma was here. I get back in the bed and I grip the blanket that she made for me, holding onto it like a life jacket.*

My memory rushes in like a tsunami destroying every living and breathing thing in its path. I am carried away with a violent wave that ushers me into a deep depression. I am trying to swim against the fierce current, striving with every stroke of my arms and kick of my legs to forget again the vile things I am remembering. Not that I could fail to remember mind you, but I have tried not to every day of my life for the past thirty years. This time, I remember as I have never remembered before.

Memories—old, nasty, vicious, corroded, unwelcome memories—are pressing in on every side of my mind. My head is exploding like an angry volcano from the pressure, spouting out memories all around me. I'm drowning. I'm drowning in my memories. I don't think that I am going to make it out of the dark place I've entered.

As a child of five or six, I had a pretty normal curiosity about sex. I had heard a little about it, I had asked a little about it, and I had walked in on my mother and george once or twice, enough to have my curiosity raised.

I remember being introduced to "playing doctor," as we called it with friends. "You show me yours and I'll show you mine"—you know the types of games kids play. I liked to play, too, but only up to a point. I never liked to see too much or show too much.

Once when I was playing doctor with a friend, he wanted to "operate." I did not want to go under the knife, if you know what I mean. He started sending messages through other friends that he was going to "get" me. I was so scared! I was ready to put down my stethoscope and resume my play with my baby dolls.

When we lived on Dane Street, my step-cousin Dwayne would come and visit us a lot. He liked to give me special attention. He and Derrick, his younger brother, did not have any sisters. I thought the attention was just because he liked me like a little sister. I soon found out that he had more on his mind than watching Bugs Bunny cartoons with me.

He started off lying with me on the bed as we watched television together. I must have been about five, almost six, at the time. Dwayne was about thirteen. Why I was left unsupervised with him, I don't know. Today, as the mother of my own daughter, I cannot fathom leaving her unsupervised behind a closed door with a teenage boy.

Eventually Dwayne started taking advantage of his private time with me, perhaps this was his plan all along. He began asking me to stick my hands down his pants to touch his penis. I remember that it seemed like a black abyss down there. I was curious, though, and I liked the attention he gave me. Touching his penis seemed like a small price to pay at the time. It would eventually get worse. There was a hole in my soul even as a young child. Rejection will do that for you. I was vulnerable and I craved attention. My neediness and the lack of physical protection from my father and emotional affection from my mother left me wide open...

These first lessons about sex were about to pale in comparison to the lesson I was about to receive, and trust me it was going to be a lesson I would never forget.

One afternoon when I was six years old, george asked me to take a nap with him. I don't know where my mother and Alex were, I just know that they weren't at home. It was just me and george there alone. Remember now, this is my daddy so I did not think his request unusual. I would tag along with my daddy anywhere, without a second thought, without question. I loved him with all my heart and I knew that he loved me and would never hurt me. He was my hero! I would follow him into any battle because I knew that he would protect me with his life. He knew it, too; that's why he asked.

That fateful afternoon, some thirty years ago, I walked into my mommy and daddy's bedroom as an innocent little girl. My daddy led me into that room by my little hand, which almost disappeared into his large one. The bed was made up neatly. The window shades were deviously drawn. It was a bright sunny day outside, and the sun fought against the blockage of the shade to make its way into the room casting a muffled orange glow. It was as if the sun were trying to shed light on the darkness of the dastardly deed that was dangerously approaching me, about to completely consume my unassuming being.

george lay down and had me lie beside him. I snuggled up to him. He put his arm around me. I felt safe. I felt loved. I fell asleep with a tiny smile on my face. All was right in my world.

I began to squirm around, stretch and yawn as my great awakening was set in motion. I opened my eyes and felt disoriented. I could feel that something was different, wrong, but I didn't yet know what. I could feel in my soul that the world that I woke up to was horrifically different from the world that I'd gone to sleep in.

My little mind struggled to make sense out of what was happening. But it couldn't. I felt like a building being demolished. The wrecking ball hit me without warning and I began to crumble. My foundation was shaken. It could not hold up under the great power. Before I could recover, I saw the ball coming back at me again full force. This can't be, I thought. This is wrong. I don't get it, I don't understand. I rubbed my eyes thinking that I must still be asleep, and this is all a dream. A horrible, horrible dream.

When I woke up, I was lying on top of george. He had pulled up my plaid pleated skirt-exposing my cute little flower lace—trimmed panties—and laid me on top of his erect penis. The bricks of my life came tumbling down, one by one by one by one by one. Crash!

george must have seen the strange look of alarm mixed with confusion and angst on my face.

He quickly tried to calm my fears and normalize the grotesquely abnormal by awkwardly saying, *"This is not [sex]."* Now I was young, but like I said, I had played doctor enough to know what the pussy was, and this seemed just like it to me.

I didn't know what to do or say. What is the proper thing to say or do as a six year old when you wake and find yourself laying on your daddy's erect penis? I was terrified. I was embarrassed. I was ashamed. Thoughts raced through my mind. *Can parents do this kind of thing to their kids? No, grown-ups are not supposed to touch you down there, are they?* I knew that something was terribly wrong.

I closed my eyes again. I wanted to go back to sleep and re-awaken in the world that I knew, the world that was safe. This horrifying place that I found myself in was incomprehensible, inexplicable, inconceivable, and indecipherable. My young mind could not grasp that george, my daddy, the only father that I had ever known, would do something so awful to me. The actions that george took on that day were to define the rest of my life. I wondered if he counted up the cost that I was going to have to pay for his actions.

On that ill-fated day, at six years old, my childhood ceased to exist. My little world was now disintegrated into tiny pieces. I didn't know how to put it back together again.
I looked up from the rubble into george's eyes. In the midst of this great infidelity, I longed for some glimmer of hope that everything would be like it was again. So when george swore me to secrecy, I was more than willing to comply. Not having to speak about that afternoon's ghastly events to anyone made me almost feel as if it didn't happen. The secrecy protected him, and it protected me. Not really.

On the outside I looked and sounded the same. But on the inside I would never be the same again. On the inside I was consumed with bewilderment and revulsion. I became afraid that day. From that day on, I have lived with fear every single day of my life. Every minute of every day, since I was six, I have felt unsafe and I have felt afraid.

Alex and my mother returned home later that day. I know that george had to have been petrified that I was going to tell my mother everything that happened, but there was no need for his concern. His nasty little secret was safely buried deep within my soul. I acted as if nothing had happened, because it hadn't, had it? My life was back to abnormal. I was well rested from my nap and ready to play with Alex.

To the outside world, we were the perfect family. Oh we had it made. What people did not know was that life inside of our perfect little family had metamorphosed from a butterfly into a caterpillar. It was a living hell! For me, anyway.

We all thought that george was the greatest. We all thought the best of him. Turns out we really didn't know him at all. He was an enemy. He was the worse kind of enemy, one that was safely camouflaged and dwelled masked among us.

Honestly, I cannot remember how long it was before the wrecking ball hit me again and knocked down the false wall that I had built in place of the old one that no longer stood. You would think that since he got away with it once that he would have stopped dead in his tracks. I still have blocks of times, places and things that I cannot remember. I wonder sometimes what I have forgotten when what I'm telling you is what I remember.

What I do recall is the frightful pattern that developed; george walked around our house like a voracious lion on the hunt with the taste of blood on his tongue. Slowly he crept through our house, like the tall grass plains of Africa, silently lying in wait to make his move on his unsuspecting prey; me. He devised opportunities for us to be alone; and my mother never questioned where he took me, why he took me or what he did when he took me there.

I was like a hushed sheep being led to the slaughter, for I didn't know that I had a choice about being slain. He created a cunningly calculated course of action to rip the remaining shreds of my childhood out of my hands. Step by conniving step, he began to do what I now know is common among demented adults who seek to rob the innocence of children who trust them with their lives. They try to justify their sick actions by convincing themselves that you want it just as much as they do. So they sexualize their victims.

On one of our daddy-and-daughter outings, george pulled out a magazine like I had never seen before. It had nasty-looking pictures of women with no clothes on. I couldn't believe it. He said he just wanted to show me the cartoons in the magazine. Being a kid, I liked cartoons. Unfortunately, he had to flip through and stop at all of the naked pictures on the way to the cartoons.

That son of a bitch. That selfish son of a bitch. He was willing to sacrifice my body, soul and spirit just to get his few minutes of perverse pleasure.

On many of our ventures, we would just drive around the city. He would slip one of his dry, rough hands down my pants as he drove with the other. He acted as if he owned my little body. He began to teach me about masturbation and how to do it. He told me that I should masturbate in between times with him. He wanted to make me more receptive to his sinful advances; he wanted to keep me in a state of sexualization.

I was frightened by what he was doing to me. It was all too much. I did not like the way I felt when he touched me in sexual ways. I hated it when he would ejaculate. It looked nasty and felt nasty and smelled nasty.

Now I ask myself all the time, sometimes to the point of mental exhaustion, Why did I keep silent? Why didn't I tell? First of all, no one asked. As much as I tried to act as if nothing in my life had changed, I know that someone had to see through the façade of a six-year-old girl. Secondly, my voice had been stolen and I could not find it anywhere. I wanted to scream, to holler, "Help!"—but my voice was gone. I had resolved that this was my lot in life, and I had to deal with it.

Thirdly, I instinctively knew that my silence was the glue that held my family together. I was petrified that if my mom found out, she would be destroyed. george made sure to reiterate this point to me, over and over again. *"Don't tell your mother. This would break her heart. You don't want to hurt your mother, do you?"* I didn't. I loved my mother; I didn't want to hurt her. I didn't want to see her world crumble as mine had.

Lastly, I felt like I was to blame. I thought that there must have been something that I had done wrong to bring this catastrophe upon myself. *"I must be nasty if george is doing these nasty things to me. My mom won't love me if she finds out. No one will love me if they find out. Everyone will be mad at me and tell me it's all my fault."*

I was also frightened that if I told, george would go to jail. He made sure to reiterate this point to me as well. *"If you tell anyone, they will put me in jail."* *"Well, if this is bad enough to put you in jail,"* I would think, *"why are you doing it to me?"*

You want to know what the heartbreaking truth is? As much as I hated what he was doing to me, I still loved him and did not want him to go to jail. I did not want my family to be broken apart.

At age six, I learned that people who love you hurt you. At age six, I learned that you do whatever you have to do to keep the family together. At age six, I learned that everyone else's needs were more important than mine. george needed sex from me; no matter how I felt about it, I felt like I had to. I wanted to tell my mom so that she would stop him, but I had to protect her from being hurt, so I stayed silent. I wouldn't dare tell anyone else, because then george would go to jail. So I buried the repulsive secret deep within. And there that secret stayed, decaying my tiny soul.

The abuse grew progressively worse. It all started off slowly and built to a destructive crescendo. It had begun with touching. Before long, george began to introduce me to other sexual acts to feed his unsavory, insatiable appetite for the body of his daughter, his six-, seven-, eight-year-old daughter. He introduced me to oral sex. He would masturbate into a filthy rag as he performed oral sex on me. As I got older, around eight years old, he began to try to have full-blown sexual intercourse with me. He actually tried to fit his man-sized penis into my eight-year-old vagina. It hurt so much when he tried to penetrate me; my vagina felt like it was going to burst. I would start to cry. Sometimes that would make him stop. Sometimes it wouldn't.

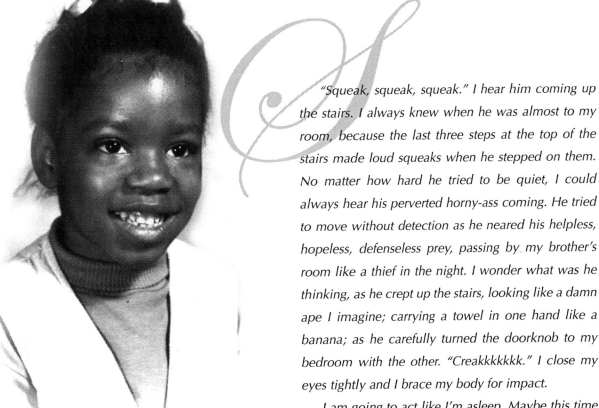

"Squeak, squeak, squeak." I hear him coming up the stairs. I always knew when he was almost to my room, because the last three steps at the top of the stairs made loud squeaks when he stepped on them. No matter how hard he tried to be quiet, I could always hear his perverted horny-ass coming. He tried to move without detection as he neared his helpless, hopeless, defenseless prey, passing by my brother's room like a thief in the night. I wonder what was he thinking, as he crept up the stairs, looking like a damn ape I imagine; carrying a towel in one hand like a banana; as he carefully turned the doorknob to my bedroom with the other. "Creakkkkkkk." I close my eyes tightly and I brace my body for impact.

I am going to act like I'm asleep. Maybe this time he will go back and get in the bed with my mother and leave me alone. I am balled up in the fetal position, trying to protect my vagina from being violated again. I still act as if I'm asleep. He turns my body and stretches out my legs, I feel him tugging at my panties...

"Lilada, Lilada! Do you hear me? What is five times seven?" my third-grade teacher asked. *"Huh?"* I responded. I had barely heard his question. I was zoned out in my own private world, where no one lived but me. My little mind was far away from A-B-C and 1-2-3. I was wondering if I would be safe tonight. I was wondering if I could sleep in peace, undisturbed, tonight. I was wondering when I would be released from my secret prison. I didn't give a damn what five times seven was; I was trying to figure out how I could make it through another night.

Not surprisingly, I developed a sleeping disorder. I still suffer with it to this day. george would come and wake me in the middle of the night to perform sexual acts on me, even on nights when I would have to get up and go to school the next morning.

The life that I lived during the day was diametrically opposed to the life I had to endure at night. My body was pillaged and raped at night by my "dad"; I then got up each morning like nothing had ever happened. My mom would help me get dressed, comb my hair, and put multicolored barrettes on my pigtails. Off I would go on the yellow school bus with Alex, as if all was right with my world.

But all was not right with my world. I had no peace, no time, no where. Fear and misery were my constant companions, every day. Would this be another day that I would be awakened at two or three in the morning and find him in my room, interrupting my sleep to pleasure himself at my expense? Would this be the day that my mom found out what had been going on for years right under her nose? Would one of my friends whom I played double-dutch and hopscotch with discover my dirty little secret today? Would I have to endure this living hell, again, today?

I learned how to disappear. No one really saw me anyway. If they had—if my mom had, if my teacher had, if my pastor had—wouldn't they have noticed how much torment I was in? Wouldn't they have helped me? No one did, so I learned to grin and bear it, suck it up, put on the façade. Living a double life was so difficult. I do not know how I managed to make it. Things did start to fall apart for me. I had a difficult time in school. Can you imagine how throughout the day my mind was totally distracted with worries about what I'd have to face when I went home? As my anxiety heightened, I became increasingly clingy with my mother. I did not want to leave her side, not even to go to school. I began to develop psychosomatic illnesses, just so that I could stay at home with my mother. I felt constantly off balance. I was stuck somewhere between the world of a child and the world an adult, yet I belonged in neither of them.

I can remember talking about sex with some of my third-grade girlfriends. They gossiped about how so-and-so had kissed this person and that person, grinded this boy and that boy. I tried to chime in with my own experiences. I knew better than to say who my partner was, but I tried to act as if I knew as much as they did. They saw me as naive, though, just an innocent, sheltered little girl; they told me I knew nothing. They laughed at my attempts to be a fast girl. Little did they know I had been exposed to more sexual experiences than they could even imagine. It is a miraculous blessing though that somehow God preserved my innocence.

There was no safe place for me anymore since george had started abusing me in our home. What was once my sanctuary became my prison, my own bedroom became my prison cell.

"Suck it, come on, suck it", his voice was low but urgently hard. His erect penis was an inch away from my mouth. I had fallen asleep in the living room, right outside my mom and george's bedroom downstairs. george woke me up in the middle of the night. I guessed I saved him the trip upstairs. He laid me on top of himself in an upside-down position, with my face toward his penis and his toward my vagina. He began to perform oral sex on me and pushed my face toward his penis.

I can remember the rank smell of his body, the foul smell of his sweaty penis, anticipating my mouth pleasuring it. With my mother asleep only steps away from us, I had been sure I would be safe from his advances. Not so. He tried to get me to have oral sex with him right there. *"Just put it in your mouth and suck it, while I do you."* Instead of teaching me what six times nine was, which he probably didn't even know himself, he was teaching me what a sixty-nine was. I was discomfited yet compliant. I put my mouth on his penis, but I could not bring myself to put it in my mouth. I could not do it.

As a child I was crazy about money. I didn't prefer to spend it; I just loved to have plenty of it. I liked to have my money crisp and clean, so I used to wash and iron it. george knew this and tried to use it to have his way with me. He used to offer me money to let him exploit my body. That sickened me. I always refused his money. I told him it made me feel like a prostitute.

When bribery with money would not work, he would use the only thing that would. He used the love and sympathy I had for him as a destructive weapon against me. When I refused his sexual advances, he would sometimes actually start to cry. He would tell me that he couldn't go to work with an erect penis, because the guys at work would make fun of him. I began to feel that it was my duty to do what my mother would not do.

What an asshole! I wish that he would have just beaten the shit out of me to get me to yield to his desires instead of poisoning love for me by using my love for him as a weapon against me. I grew up believing that I had to suck up and do shit to satisfy those that I loved. This is a lesson that I would take into future relationships that would cost me a great deal.

My parents were having marital problems. No shit, huh? I don't know when their relationship began to go sour, but it did, and it was rank. I suppose they were like most couples: things don't get bad all at once, the decline is gradual. They had the ups and downs of most couples, but after a while, there were more downs than ups.

Guess who got the inside scoop? Yeah, me! So not only was I dragged in way over my head into an adult sexual relationship with my "father," but I was also privy to the personal details of their relationship, on all levels. He would actually have a conversation with me about their sex life. That was way too much information. What was I supposed to do with all of that information as a child? I felt like I was disintegrating. I began to resent my mother; thinking that if she was doing what she was supposed to do, I wouldn't have to.

I began to be repulsed by the sight, the smell, and the sound of the voice of the man I once loved unconditionally.

"Come here, Lil, I want to show you something." george called me into his bedroom. We were at home alone together, again. I was older now, maybe ten. The room looked eerie, the same as it did that first unspeakable afternoon. Again the shades were drawn, and the sun did its best but was rendered powerless against the insanity. I didn't know what to expect besides the usual. I don't know how he expected me to react as his clammy hands pulled a pile of nude Polaroid pictures of me out of his shirt pocket and gave them to me. Maybe he wanted me to autograph them. He had taken these pornographic pictures of me when I was asleep. He had been carrying them around with him God only knows how long. I wondered if he had shown them to others. I felt an even deeper level of betrayal.

I really can't find the words to fully express how I felt when I saw those pictures. To say that I was shocked, revolted, and enraged would be a grotesque understatement. To say that I felt like a filthy piece of ass would be an underestimation. I couldn't believe my eyes. I was so embarrassed and so ashamed. I wanted to go run and lock myself away in a deep, dark, dank dungeon. Then I realized that I was already in one.

I could not believe what that sick son of a bitch had done to me. Please don't get me wrong, it's not as if all of the unforgivable things he had already done weren't a repulsive atrocity. It was just something about seeing it in pictures. Viewing my naked little body lying there with my skirt pulled-up and my panties pulled down around my ankles made what I had tried for years to convince myself wasn't really happening to me, real. I looked so vulnerable. I cried when I looked at myself in those pictures. My heart broke for my own self.

To others, george was one of the nicest guys you would ever meet. If you met him today, you would like him. If I were to tell this story to people who know him, they would call me a liar! Some already have. To them all I have to say is, I wish I were lying. I really wish I were.

To endure the obliteration of my childhood, I created an imaginary dream world. While he had his way with my body, my mind went far away. Sometimes it felt as if I had left my body. I would float close to the ceiling, looking down on him and what he was doing to me as if it were someone else. Then I would fly away off to my own world. A world where no one could harm me. A world of beautiful things I could only imagine.

I constantly felt odd, awkward, out of place. I felt as if I wore the scarlet letter A. My letter stood for "abused." While I clung to my secrecy like a drowning person who was just thrown a life line, I still felt as if everyone around me could see that I was tainted. I feared that they could look into my eyes and see the scars on my soul. I withdrew and become very shy and introverted. I avoided group events like classmates' parties, Girl Scouts, and after-school clubs, unless I was with my big brother.

Believe it or not, george and Dwayne were not the only ones to whom my mother allowed free access to me. I was like a lost sheep in the company of ravenous wolves. Where was my mother?

I'm sure that as the abuse with george progressed, it impacted my behaviors and attitudes in many ways. There's no way that a child can become sexualized at such a young age and for such a long duration and there be no evidence. It's just not possible. So I suppose as I developed it caught the attention of others. I was now more needy and vulnerable than ever before.

My premature development, though undetected by my mother, caught the attention of a few by-standers who were more than happy to address the issue at hand.

My step-cousin Dwayne was still in the picture. One night when we were living on Fisher

Street, george and my mother threw another one of their infamous house parties. Several friends and family members were there. My aunt Dorothy brought Dwayne with her. There were a couple of other kids there, too. We were all banished to my parents' bedroom; yes, the notorious bedroom. We were to go to sleep while the card playing, loud laughing, and heavy drinking went deep into the night.

I was the only girl lying in the bed with enough boys to make a basketball team. The lights were off, the door was closed, the music was loud, and the booze was plenteous. Dwayne, being one of the boys in the room, maximized this opportunity and laid right next to me. While I was asleep, he attempted to rape me. He must have been around fifteen by this time, and his sexual appetite was more voracious than it was upon our last encounter. I woke up to a sharp feeling of pain in my vagina. Dwayne had long, sharp fingernails, and he was using them to find my opening so that he could penetrate me with his penis. It hurt so badly. I wanted to scream out for help, but by this time I was far too conditioned to silent suffering and secrecy to say a mumbling word.

He kept trying and trying to force his penis into my vagina, but it was too small for him to fully penetrate me. I was so afraid. I did not know what to do. There were others in the same bed—my brother, my cousin John—but they were just kids. I didn't think they could do anything to help me. Plus, I felt ashamed. I felt as if there was something I had done, something about me that made men act this way. It was my fault. Telling on him would be telling on me. Something was wrong with me. So, I lay there like road kill and allowed him to have his way with me.

Just when I was about to be conquered by my step-cousin, an unlikely hero stepped in to save me: george came through the door like Indiana Jones busting into the Temple of Doom and called Dwayne out. He told him he was too old to be in there lying on the bed with us kids. I guess george was afraid that Dwayne might try to get a piece of the ass that he claimed as his own. God forbid that should happen. I guess george wanted to keep me all to himself.

When I was around seven years old, my mother accepted Christ as her Lord and Savior, so she thought it proper to begin attending church again. We began going to a little white church on Williamson Street. A nice pastor from Milwaukee would drive up every Sunday. At the church we met Deacon Sherman and Brother Cal. They taught Sunday school and assisted the pastor in many other church-related duties. We attended there for a few years. The attendance was only about ten on a good Sunday, so we all got to know one another very well. Alex and I were the only kids who attended on a regular basis. Sometimes Brother Cal would bring his two kids who were a little younger than we were.

Deacon Sherman took a special interest in me. Hummm, I wonder why? I saw him as the grandfather figure I had been missing all my life. He had to be in his late sixties or early seventies. He would ask my mother if he could spend time with me. Unbelievably, she would let me go with him, alone. I didn't protest. I wanted to spend time with him. Feeling deprived of attention and the expression of love from my mother, I wanted someone to really see me. It seemed as if Deacon Sherman did. The so-called love I received from george was now tainted. I was still on my journey.

He would take me to the farmers' market on Saturdays and out for long drives. On one of our drives, my hopes of his being a grandfather to me were dashed. Back in those days (not too long ago), before airbags, kids could sit in a car's front seat with or without a seatbelt. That day I was sitting shotgun. I felt like a big girl, and I guess that I must have looked like one to Deacon Sherman. As we drove down the street, he put his old, wrinkled hand on my young tender thigh, no longer innocent, and rubbed it.

I thought to myself, "*You have got to be kidding. Not you too, Grandpa? What is it with me that brings this out in men?*" I wondered so desperately. I continued to look out the window as if nothing had happened. Looking at the people and the world around me that seemed so normal, I wished that I was part of their world.

He told me not to tell anyone. He didn't have to worry about that; my mouth was sealed shut with super glue on such matters. Fortunately, a sense of right must have overtaken him before he went any further, because I do not remember his ever trying anything again.

When we began to have church in our home, Brother Cal joined us there and served as a deacon. My mom would let him come upstairs to play with my brother and me in our room. He would tickle me and feel my chest (let me remind you that I had no chest). It did not feel right, but I was too conditioned as a victim to know what to do about it.

Brother Cal owned a farm. One day he invited our family out for a fun day of recreation there. Alex and I had grown up in the city and had never had the "down south" experience, because all our close relatives lived up north. The thought of going to a real farm and seeing live animals was thrilling!

I got to see a pig—no, I think that big old thing had to be a hog- up close and in person for the first time. I could not believe that anything could smell as bad as that pig did. As much as I loved bacon, after meeting that pig, I had to take a bit of a break from pork.

Brother Cal also had horses. I was so excited that I would get to ride one for the first time in my life. I was too small to ride the horse by myself, so he said I could ride with him. I was glad, because I was a bit afraid as well as excited. He saddled up the horse, got on, and then pulled me up on the saddle in front of him. We began at a slow trot and then galloped a little, I squealed with excitement and a bit of fright.

Then something seemed odd, wrong. Brother Cal began to press himself up against my bottom. There was something hard between him and me. It didn't feel right—something inside told it was wrong. I now know that he got an erection rubbing up against me. My mother was standing by, watching me ride the horse and smiling at us, waving as we rode by.

For some odd reason, I later told my mother about some of the things that Brother Cal, used to do. I am not sure why I told her about Cal, but not about george. Perverted loyalty? Maybe? I have heard that sometimes children who are being abused will do this. They will tell a little bit of what seems safe to say in hopes of the adults taking the initiative to delve deeper. Had my mother, at this time, asked me if anyone else had done something inappropriate to me, I would have told her. This was some time after he stopped coming to our church. I can remember her saying that she should tell george. Ha-Ha!

When I look back and think that all of this desecration of my body, mind and soul—at the hands of three trusted men and one horny teenager—all happening at the same time, I wonder how I did not completely lose my mind. I went on with life as usual, but day by day, week by week, bits of my soul were dying. I did not lose my mind, but I did lose my spirit.

I felt ashamed of myself all the time. I had to deal with those feelings all alone. No one could see my pain, no one felt my shame. I was left alone to deal with it all. I don't know how it was possible for no one to see what was going on. Surely someone could see that the brightness had left my eyes. Surely someone could see that pain was overtaking me. Surely someone could see the innocence of my childhood slipping away.

I lost all hope at this point in my young life. By the age of ten I had already endured the miseries of a great-grandmother. I couldn't imagine overcoming the adversities of my past and enjoying a joyful, productive, and fulfilling life. I was tainted and spoiled rotten to the bone.

I was furious with myself. I took the pain that others caused me and turned it inward. I had no idea that I was not the one with the problem, that I was not the one who should be carrying guilt and shame. I did not realize that I was not to blame. But blame myself is what I did. I blamed myself for everything.

I thought that if I had been prettier, a better daughter, a son instead of a daughter, a better student, a better person, then I would not have been polluted. I figured there must have been something I did wrong to deserve my life.

That is a heavy burden to carry—pain, shame, and blame for something that was never my fault. But I did carry it. That burden weighed me down more and more with every step I took. I felt used, abused, and good-for-nothing. I was ruined. I was no longer proper for any good thing, or so I thought.

The force of the abuse permeated every aspect of my life, like red Kool-Aid spilled on white carpet. It spread every-where, and no amount of scrubbing could remove the stain it left on my soul. The impact went to the very core of my being.

Every experience I had, good or bad, every relationship, everything I did, passed through the filter of my abuse and was contaminated. The abuse dictated how I felt about myself. I was ashamed of what had been done to me, and I was ashamed of who I was. I grew to hate myself and everything that made me, me.

I assumed others saw me as dreadful, appalling and nasty. Though I kept the secret of the abuse clenched deep within, I was sure that people could look through me and see the blem-ishes on my soul.

As years went by, I grew in knowledge of God myself, and even though I was in the church, saved and sanctified, I didn't want to allow even God to see the corrosion embedded deep in my core essence. I wanted to keep it all buried. If it ever came out, I would be destroyed. I was dying and no one gave a damn about it.

Lilada Gee

Where was my mother during all of these sexual transactions, you might wonder. She was literally often no more than a few feet away; she just had her eyes closed and her ears plugged. Like the three little monkeys, she heard nothing, saw nothing and spoke nothing.

Chapter Seven
Shame On Me!

Where Can I Take My Shame?

Where can I take my shame,
when those around me ignore my pain?

Where can I take my shame,
when deep inside me I feel that I'm to blame?

My innocence is gone; I no longer believe
that good is inside
Only disgust, despair and degradation reside

I was lost, lonely, drowning, I felt invisible
I need someone to rescue me, make my life livable

I've closed my heart to truth, resolved to live a lie
Some days it seems easier to just curl up and die!

My life—is this how I was predestined to be?
So many things distort my view, my true self
I no longer see

Feeling unworthy of peace, I settle for a life full of pain
Rejecting God's definition of me, I willingly embrace my shame

Still in the deep darkness, within my prison walls,
A voice, a deeper knowing, inside to my soul calls

It paints a vision of my true self that I cannot yet see,
It's difficult to grasp because of my false definition of me

This false definition keeps me from being set free,
Once imposed by others, now it is imposed by me

I want to feel better, do better, be better, but I end up feeling the same
When I try to escape my prison,
I pull myself back in with the strong arms of my own shame.

What am I doing here? I want to get out. I wonder if I can get out of here? Wait a minute, I know better than that. I don't know why I am asking myself that stupid question. I know that here is right where I am supposed to be. I don't know what I was thinking.

I have spent most of my life at the bottom of a deep, dark pit, drowning in my own shit. I am sick and tired of all the shit, but as much as I hate it, I can't get away from it, and the shit won't stop coming. I have to shit; I try, but I can't keep it in. I have nowhere else to shit but all around myself. I can see the opening at the top of the pit, but it is far away from my reach. I try to climb out by standing on my shit—this shit has got to be good for something—but it offers no support, no help, for my desperate efforts to escape. The walls are slimy, and every time I try to climb them, I fall right back down into the stinky pile of shit. People walk by, and I yell to get their attention, but they don't see me, they don't hear me. All they do is smell the pile of shit, and are repelled by it. They assume that this is just a shit hole, so they send their own shit down into the pit, and it mixes with mine.

This is shame. This is my life of shame.

Shame caused me to live in dark, dank, depressed, dejected, dismal, deprived, disadvantaged, depraved, deficient, destitute places, all my life. I know that my description of shame sounds horrible—try living there. I'd lived there for so long that I became absolutely convinced that was where I was destined to live out the rest of my days.

george was willing to do any and everything to me to fulfill his desires. He hoped somehow to satisfy the deep, demented torment of his own soul by the raping of mine.

While my friends were playing baby dolls, jump rope, and hopscotch, I was being introduced to adultery, pornography, masturbation, oral sex, and prostitution. While they were having school pictures taken, I was the subject of salacious pornographic pictures. While their dads were teaching them how to ride a bike, my dad was teaching me how to give him a blow job.

"I'll give you ten dollars if you let me kiss it. Please let me kiss it!" george was on the floor of my bedroom on his knees, begging me to allow him access to my body. "Kiss it" is what he called it. It almost sounds sweet and innocent, doesn't it? He was holding a rag in his hand as he begged, prepared to masturbate into it as he performed oral sex on me.

"No!" I yelled. *"Leave me alone!"* I didn't have the emotional strength to deal with this shit today. I was tired, weary. I just wanted to be a regular kid like all my friends. They were outside playing, and I was in my room being introduced to the evil world of prostitution.

"I'll give you twenty dollars!" I was eight years old, and this man was offering me money for sexual favors. Just when I thought it could not get any worse, it did. As nasty as I already felt, I felt even nastier.

"I'm not a prostitute!" I would yell at him. Emotional manipulation and a desire to protect my mother would persuade me, but hell no, I wasn't going to do it for money.

You would think that the sexual abuse itself would have been enough. But it wasn't. I would swear that george was out to destroy me. Did he think that I was his saving grace? Did he feel that he could survive only if he sucked all the life out of me? I, who was once his loving and devoted daughter, had become little more than a pussy to him.

I believe that when you have sexual contact with someone, more than just a physical exchange takes place. I think there is a transfer between souls. george's having sex with me opened me up to all the sexual deviance he carried in his soul. The spirit of everyone he had ever been with, including my mother, was transferred to me. Their hurts, their pains, their perversions, insecurities, unfulfilled dreams—I could feel the weight of it all on my tiny soul, and it was too much to take.

My flesh crawled when he touched me. His hands were dry and rough against my tender skin. He did not touch me with the loving hands of the father that I needed, but with the desperate, violent hands of an obsessive maniac. He was like a wild, hungry dog with fresh kill.

He would provide all kinds of sexual "instruction." Once he got a mirror so that I could look at my vagina while he attempted to partially penetrate it with his penis. I remember seeing my vagina turn red. He told me that by doing this, he could make me get my period. He told me that if he sucked my breasts—the tiny nipples on my flat girl-chest—they would get really big.

He would abuse me in the car, in my bedroom with my brother asleep in the other bed, in the living room with my mother asleep in the next room, in the basement. He abused me here and there, he abused me anywhere. The place didn't matter, just as long as he could get his crusty hands on me.

I learned how to make it through. I learned how to absent myself from my body, to cut off my feelings, emotions, preferences, wants and needs. (What I didn't know was how to turn them back on again.) I used to have recurring dreams of a secret room hidden in the wall of our kitchen. Whenever I was sad or afraid, or was being desecrated by george, I would "go there" in my mind. This secret room was a little girl's dream. It was beautiful, full of baby dolls and candy. Most of all, it was safe. No one else knew it was there.

I wasn't prepared to handle what was happening to me. How could I have been? None of this should have ever happened. I wasn't ready! My body wasn't ready. My mind wasn't ready. I didn't know how to handle sexual arousal. It was physically overwhelming. My spirit wasn't ready. My spirit wasn't strong enough yet to deal with this. My soul wasn't ready. I didn't have the emotional maturity to deal with the continual assaults and manipulation. I should not have even known what sex was, let alone be in the predicament I was in. I was terribly confused. The question, What did I do to deserve this? haunted me.

The feelings, the emotions and the arousal were excruciating. But at the same time it felt pleasurable. I didn't understand how a bad thing could feel good. The first time I had an orgasm, I felt like I was going to explode from the physical eruption in my body. I didn't know how to respond. All I could do was cry.

After that I would often have orgasms when george performed oral sex on me or manually stimulated my clitoris. I hated my body for responding to his abuse. It was the most pain and the most pleasure I had ever felt in my young life, and I was feeling them both at the same time. I could not forgive my body for betraying me and making me a part of my own torment. I wondered what kind of person I could be to feel any pleasure at all in george's touch. The guilt and shame I felt from feeling pleasure in the exploitation of my body pushed me further down into the pit of shame. I grew to loathe myself and my body. I was disgusted and I felt disgusting.

As the sexual abuse progressed, my body began to yearn for the pleasure that the sexual stimulation yielded. It's horrifying to admit, but it is true. Once I had become sexually aroused, my body began to crave more. The agonizing pleasure I felt from the orgasm was like an addictive drug to my ailing soul. My body had been awakened before it was time.

Sometimes when I was alone in my room, feeling overwhelmed by my life's pressures, I would pacify myself by masturbating, just as george had taught me to do. Any pleasure that I felt was always mixed with pungent feelings of self-hatred and repugnance. When I masturbated, I would go for the orgasm, but as soon as I had it, I was enveloped by repulsion of myself. The pure pleasure God intended for sex to bring to two loving people had been terribly corrupted. I began to abuse myself by inserting all kinds of objects into my vagina in my attempts to achieve punishment and pleasure. One no longer came without the other. I could not enjoy pleasure of any kind without pain. If I could not cause myself physical pain, then I caused myself emotional pain through the mental aguish of self-defeating, destructive and dangerous thoughts. I did not need the judgment for anyone else, my own thoughts damned me.

One day I was feeling sexually aroused. I must have been about nine years old, so the sexual abuse had been going on for three years. This time, the stalked went and looked for the stalker. I went and looked for george. I found him in the basement. I didn't come right out and ask for it, but I gave him the message that I wanted him to perform oral sex on me. He almost fell over himself to oblige. *"Just let me know anytime you want me to do it,"* he told me, drooling out of the side of his mouth as he spoke those iniquitous words.

It is very difficult for me to tell this story; it's such an awful and disgraceful truth. After that day, I felt bound by the shame, guilt, and regret of this act. Looking back on it, I felt that single action gave george the message I had wanted it all along: that what he was doing was as much for me as it was for him. I felt I had sold my soul to the devil that day. At that point there was transference of shame. I felt that everything was all my fault.

Of course the stimulation wasn't what I really wanted. My body craved it, and I didn't know how to control those demands. I was like a little baby born to a crack-addicted mother. The baby doesn't realize the devastation that crack has already brought to her young life; all she knows is there's something she badly wants and thinks she needs. She has no idea that the thing she yearns for is the cause of this pain.

This was my secret within my secret. I really did not want to include it in this book. I have been too ashamed to tell this part of my story to anyone. Over the years, I have told my story to others, but part of me remained bound by this most secret shame. That man tried to make me his whore. He made me crave what I should not have even tasted. That son of a bitch twisted and misshaped my whole life.

It wasn't my fault. I now know that on a cognitive level; it's my soul that has a hard time understanding this truth. I was a child. george was an adult. Even if I had totally undressed and begged him to "give it to me," it was his responsibility to protect me and do what was right. He should have known better and should have done better by me.

My craving for sex was premature and misdirected. My physical response to arousal during the vandalizing of my body was no more than my body's reflexive response. It was in no way a license for george to defile me. It was not an acceptance of the abuse; it was a result of the abuse. The abnormal use of sex taught me to use it incorrectly. What I needed and truly desired was the love and affection of parents who could get the hell over themselves enough to stop screwing me (literally and figuratively) and parent me.

The residual effects of the abuse came out with others, not just with george. I began to act out sexually with kids from the neighborhood. Back then, we used birth control that offered 100% protection every time; it was called "bumping and grinding." That was as far as I would go; I was afraid to have actual sexual intercourse with anyone. As a matter of fact, if one of my little boyfriends pushed too much to go all the way, I cut him off from the bump and grind.

Had it not been for the grace of God, I would have become a statistic like many other young women who suffered as I have. By all accounts, I should have been on drugs, having sex with the first and last boy I found and everyone in between, and been a teen parent.

That doesn't mean there had been no impact, of course. It was just on the down low, deep down where I stuffed it, hoping that I could get rid of it without anyone seeing it. But that was like throwing raw chicken in a trashcan. It is out of sight, but wait a day or two. An unbearable aroma will permeate every crack and crevice of your house and just about kill you.

Later, my relationship with my husband Duane triggered the craving again. My feelings for him overwhelmed me emotionally and physically. We did not have sexual intercourse, before we were married, but we did a lot of around-the-course, if you know what I mean. I knew better, but it seemed like the thing to do at the time. I allowed my vagina to dictate my actions, and it led me directly to more secrets, more shit and more shame.

My marriage to Duane blew the roof off it all. When I had sex with my husband and had an orgasm, the familiar feelings of self-hatred and disgust would come over me. I assumed it was just Duane and I in the bed, but it wasn't. I could not get the vile things george did to me out of my mind. It was as if he was right there with us. When Duane touched me, it was george's hands that I felt touch me. When Duane kissed me, it was george's lips that I felt kiss me.

In addition to the emotional and spiritual revulsion, my body rejected sexual intercourse. I had a physiological response to sexual intercourse. It physically hurt to have sex. I would complain about it to my gynecologist, but there was no medical reason for the pain; it was just another psychosexual leftover from the abuse.

Unfortunately for my husband, he got a lot of the residual rage that george deserved. Having sex with Duane was a torturous pleasure. I was plagued by nightmares (I still am) and flashbacks. (I still have those, too. As I write this chapter, I have had a flashback of george ejaculating on my clitoris as he masturbated over me. It felt nasty and slimy. I had forgotten that and so many other things. I hate that I remembered that.) The abuse continued to haunt my days and my nights.

As the emotional and verbal abuse escalated in our marriage, it became even more difficult for me to have sex with Duane. On an unconscious level, I think I welcomed the abuse, because it gave me an excuse to not have to make love. It became a vicious cycle of pain that was a means to an end. Once again sex, pain and pleasure were entangled for me. I didn't know where one began and the other ended. They were the same to me, and they all made me feel like shit.

I don't understand why sexual abuse has such a profound impact on a life. Its disastrous collision has touched every area of my life. There is nothing about me that has not been violated by its devastation.

For years, I blamed myself for not telling. I felt shame for my secrecy and silence. So why did I keep silent?

I hate to ask that question, but I have to. I no longer believe the abuse was my fault—or that abuse is the fault of any child, on any level. I ask so that I can protect my children from ever being in that place. I ask so that I can help a mother recognize that same desperation in her own child, so that she can help her child before it's too late.

Fear? Yes, fear was definitely a reason. I was afraid my whole world would come crashing down around me. Little did I realize that it already had. Did I want love? Yes, I did. My abuser gave me the "love" and attention that I needed from my mother and my own damned father. If either one of them had been on their job, I would not have been prey to that sick animal.

Validation? There was a sense of validation. I felt valuable because he saw me. Outside of the sexual predation, he was nice to me. As you might imagine, he gave me whatever I wanted in order to keep me happy, keep me silent. So it seemed as if I had the best dad in the world, one who would do anything for me. The truth, of course, was that he would do anything *to* me.

My mother? Yes, I wanted to protect my mother. My silence was the ultimate sacrifice and ploy for her love. I felt I was doing her a favor. In some twisted but innocent way, I believed that by doing what she would not do, I was helping to keep her husband around. If he were messing with me, he wouldn't hurt my mother by leaving her for another woman.

Love? I did love him and didn't want him to suffer. I felt like I was helping him. He was in pain, in need, and I could do something about it. All I had to do was lie there until he was done. Don't get me wrong; I hated every second of every moment of it. But at the time it seemed like a small price to pay for the result.

I had never intended to ever tell anyone about the abuse. After I told my mother, that was as far as I intended to go. It was my plan to go to the grave with this secret. I was mortified by the thought of others knowing my undisclosed shame. I didn't even tell my mother all the truth. She didn't ask, I didn't tell. As long as I kept the secret, it kept me bound to george in the darkness.

Shame is one of the most destructive emotions. I thought that secrecy was my saving grace, because if no one knew, at least I could seem like more than I thought that I was. Secrecy was ultimately my damnation, because it prolonged my prison sentence.

Shit happens! There's no way around it in this world. It happens to all of us in one way or another. If it hasn't happened to you yet, keep living. Shit leads us to embrace shame, and shame leads us directly to secrecy, which leads to more shit, more shame, and more secrecy. It becomes a vicious cycle; which leads to more shit, more shame, and more secrecy. Which leads to more shit, more shame and, more secrecy, which leads to...

Shame gets its power from secrecy. Secrecy distorts the truth. Truth and honesty destroy the secrets, which in turn destroy the shame. When secrecy and shame are gone, you can clearly see which shit is yours and which shit belongs to someone else. It's always easier to clean up your own shit when you can distinguish yours from everyone else's. I am working on cleaning up mine; I have learned to let others clean up theirs.

As much as I fought against it, truth was my ticket to freedom. I was terrified, but deep inside, I understood that telling the truth was not just something I could do, it was what I had to do. I began to share my story with women I knew had gone through sexual abuse. Oddly enough, instead of feeling like more shit, I began to feel better. So I told the story more often, and I began to feel even better. I became strong enough to give my testimony at church. I stood in mortal fear as I addressed the audience of men and women of Fountain of Life Family Worship Center and told them about my crazy-ass life.

There was another result, more amazing than my feeling better. Over the years that I have shared my testimony of survival, countless women have approached me and told me that my honesty was freeing them. Who would have thought it?

All the old shit, shame, and secrets were keeping me bound to the past. Truth was setting me free, releasing me from the bondage that was forged in disgrace. I still had a few more roads to travel, though, before I had won a total victory over shame.

Chapter Eight
Mommy Dearest

How?

How could a man I loved so much,
use my pure love for him against me?

All he did was fulfill his own sinful lusts,
as he destroyed what my future would be.

How could you, my own mother,
who professed your love for me to the world,

Turn a deaf ear and a blind eye to the pain,
that raged inside of your little girl?

How could you kiss again the lips that your husband
used to violate my vagina that was innocent?

How could the hands that ravaged my body before
I even knew it myself, touch you again?
To me this makes no sense

How could you again desire inside of you
the penis your husband used to almost burst my tiny vagina?

Mom, did you hear all of the vile things I told you he did to me?
You act as if all of this is minor

How could you, Mom, do to me what your mother did to you?
Isn't this, when you were a little girl, what you swore you would never do?

I have no answers, just painful questions.
Mom, how could this be?

I can't believe you allowed what was done to you,
Also happen to me

How, Mom, how?

My mother, like her mother before her and perhaps her mother before her, was either unable or unwilling to deal with her own self, shame, secrets and shit. When I was born, I inherited all of her unresolved, unfaced, unworked-on, undealt-with, unconfronted, unhealed, unprayed-on, unspoken issues. I paid the price for them all, just as she had for her mother's issues before her. This is what happens to your children and your children's children when you don't deal with your own damned shit.

This is probably the most difficult part of this book to write. Writing honestly and without reservation about one's relationship with one's mother is a vast and tangled challenge. As I write, I am still healing.

My mother was my hero. I thought she knew everything, I thought she could do anything, and I thought she would protect me from anyone who might even just think about trying to hurt my brother or me. I thought that she would always care for and protect me from the evil that lurked about in the world. She did. What she did not do was protect me from the evil that lurked about in our own home.

⚜

I looked into my mother's eyes to find out who I was. I needed to know the definition of myself. I wanted to know that she loved me; I wanted to know that I was important to her; I wanted to know if she saw me. Once I even asked her what she saw when she looked at me? I wanted to know. I craved her acceptance and her approval.

She was the strongest woman I had ever known. She always seemed to know what to say, what to do, when to do it and everything that everyone else should do, too. She always had the right answer, the right solution, the right method. In my eyes, my mother could do no wrong. Even when I sensed that her love for Alex was different—greater—than her love for me, I didn't fault her for that. I just assumed there was something wrong with me. I thought maybe it was because I was a girl. I thought maybe it was because she hadn't been married to my father. She never talked about him to me. It was always the Gees this and the Gees that, like it was the best thing in the world to be a Gee, and I knew that I was a Gee in name only. So I tried even harder to get her attention.

When we were kids, we used to play the game "Mother May I?" It is similar to "Simon Says." Before you can make a move, you have to ask the permission of the "mother." If you don't ask or if she says no, any move that you make is illegal and will get you kicked out of the game. If the "mother" says yes, you can boldly do or say the thing that you requested.

Children, especially girl children, look to their mothers to find out who they are and what they may or may not do or become. In many ways our mothers serve as our own reflections. We look at the image of the path our mother's life has taken, and we imagine what our life will be.

After the abuse began, I wanted to tell my mother what was going on, but I could not bring myself to tell her or anyone else my deep dark secret. I felt so ashamed. george would often warn me that it would kill my mother if she found out what was going on. Protecting my mother from the ugly truth meant more to me than protecting myself. But the day would finally come when the weight of the life that I was enduring out-weighed my desire to protect my mother.

I was full of terror, trepidation and tears on the day I revealed to my mother that george had been sexually abusing me. Earlier that day george had asked me to take a ride with him. I knew what "take a ride with me" meant. I refused to go with him. I couldn't do it. I didn't know what was going to happen when I told her, but by then I knew what would happen if I didn't, and I was more afraid of that. That day I knew I could not go on one more second of one more minute of one more hour of one more day, of one more week of one more year, being at the beck and call of george's unsavory lusts. The abuse had been rapidly progressing. He had already begun trying to insert the head of his penis into the petite opening of my young vagina. Before long, I knew, george would attempt full-blown sexual intercourse with me.

Whether it was summer or winter I don't recall, but I do remember that sunshine was streaming through our living-room window casting rays of light on everything it hit. One of those rays hit me like a lightening bolt. It was time for me to shine the light on what had been going on for far too long. My body was shaking from bearing the weight of the great task that was before me. I could feel my heart beating outside of my chest. I thought that my heart was going to burst right out of my shirt. I looked down at the ground as I talked to her; I was too ashamed to look her in her face. I counted the strands on our shag carpeting as I attempted to get out the words that I had been choking to death on for five long years.

As I struggled to gain my composure, the words came flying out of mouth like bullets shot from a pistol. They escaped my lips faster than I could stop them.

I told her. She believed me. She embraced me. She protected me. I openly wept in her arms the silent tears that I had suppressed for five long and damaging years. We wept together. I exhaled a sigh of relief. I had a great sense of freedom and safety.

Verline kicked george out of the house that same day. Everything seemed perfect. My mother talked about the situation like it was she and I against him, against the world. I thought we were co-victims and co-warriors. It felt so good to share the secret that kept me in isolation. It was still shit that we were dealing with, but I felt like we were in this shit together. That night I slept in my mother's bed and fell asleep in her arms. I slept through the night for the first time in years. I could not have wanted more. It was finally over; this long treacherous ordeal was finally over. I could go on to live a life free of sin and shame, free of guilt, free of abuse. Free!

But before I had the chance to rest in my newfound peace and safety, without warning, the roof caved in on my head. One fateful afternoon my mother sat me down and told me that george would be coming back to live with us. I felt as if she had just pushed me out of the plane without a parachute. I knew that I was going to hit the ground and be shattered. I felt more alone than I had ever felt in my life.

The day that my mother allowed george to move back into the house with our family, I lost all sense of self. If I'd had any self-worth left, I lost it on that ill-fated day. I would never again feel safe in my world. I had no place to call home. I retreated to my room, which became my hiding place.

I was perplexed, bewildered, disturbed, saddened, disappointed, furious, terrified. I felt as if I didn't really exist. I became a shell; the life inside of me was gone. What would my life be like now? I couldn't understand it, didn't want it, but as an eleven-year-old there was nothing I knew to do to stop it, so I resolved that I'd have to live with it.

I could in no way conceive how my mother could even begin to consider taking back this sick depraved "man"—back into our lives, back into our home, back into her bed. In my quest for comprehension of an incomprehensible situation, I have finally realized that there is no answer, no reason, no excuse that will ever quench my desire to understand why my mother did what she did to me, to us.

What my mother did to me was an awful, agonizing, and appalling, abusive act that I would have to pay for the rest of my life. What my mother did to me was unfair, unkind, unspeakable, unbearable, unloving, uncaring, un-Christian, un-mother-like, unthinkable, unrighteous, un-American. What my mother did to me was an act of violence.

Why? The easy and the obvious answer would be because it's what she saw her mother do, but doesn't it at the same time seem like that would be the reason why she wouldn't have? Surely it should have been enough to know that a grown man, who happened to be her husband, had tried to put his man-sized dick into my young virgin vagina. You would think that finding out that he had been abusing me for five years, right under her nose, would have been enough. I don't know; maybe I am the one who's wrong. Forgive and forget, right?

What would it take for my mother to rescue me? She was sensitive to everyone else's pain. What else could I conclude but that I didn't matter, my feelings didn't matter, my utter disgrace didn't matter—I did not matter? How could I have worth if my mother didn't give it to me? If I didn't matter to my own mother, who could I matter to in this world? My father—my real father? Well, he wasn't in the picture to tell me any differently. To him, I wasn't important enough to be worth the time to get to know.

Over the years my mom and I have talked about many of these issues. I wrote earlier that I love my mother. I longed for her attention, love and acceptance, yet she has never really seen me. I feel as if I have always been invisible to her.

⁂

There is something that bothers me about the day I told my mother about the abuse. As I now reflect upon it, I remember that my mother did not act shocked. She was calm, cool, and collected. There were no, "oh my gods!" or "you must be kiddings!" She didn't even raise her voice. I'm telling you right now, had my eleven-year-old daughter just told me that my husband had been having sex with her, somebody's ass was going to get kicked right then and right there. I would have hollered, screamed, cussed, cried, grabbed a knife, a gun or something, and raised holy hell. But she was composed, even when she called george in to question him about my allegations. She questioned him like she was asking him whether or not he forgot to take out the trash. You know now that I think back on that moment, my mother's reaction really disturbs me. I am not sure how to interpret her response. It was almost like it was the confirmation to something that she already suspected. Though I do not believe my mother consciously knew that george was sexually abusing me over the course of those five years, I do ask myself over and over again how she couldn't see that her daughter was dying, day by day by day.

My mother told me years later that there was something about the look on my face when I refused to go with george that day. Well, hell, hadn't I had that look on my face for five years? Had she looked at me? Had she seen me at all the last five years? Hadn't she seen that I was wasting away, dying right under her nose? Couldn't she smell the revolting stench of my decomposing soul? Couldn't she smell the stench of her husband on me? Couldn't she see the dark circles under my eyes from the lack of sleep? Couldn't she see the look of anxiety and terror on my face? Couldn't she see me becoming a recluse, shying away from my friends? Couldn't she see the same look on my face that she used to see reflected in her own image?

Many people say that I am the spitting image of my mother—that I look like her, act like her, and sound like her on the phone. Yet with all of our similarities, I was still indiscernible to her. She never really looked at me enough to see me. There I was in her own home, her only daughter, suffering, dying inside, and she never looked at me long enough and hard enough to see me. It is not that she isn't an empathic and compassionate person; she is. Outside of the family she was very aware of others' suffering and pain and would attempt to rescue them. She was constantly trying to rescue my cousin, who had a tumultuous relationship with her mother, my mother's younger sister Bessie. My mother saw her pain and stepped in to rescue my cousin from the hellish torture she had been enduring in her home, even at the risk of losing her relationship with her baby sister in the midst of the battle.

Lilada Gee

It's not that she's clueless. My mother is a very intuitive person; I told you, she always has the "correct" answer when others ask her what to do, and even when they don't. She saw that my step-cousin Ian, whose mother died when he was young, needed a home. My mother saw his pain and wanted to invest in him, save him, give him a better life. She invited him into our home to rescue him. Why didn't she see me and want to give me a better life?

Even after I told me mom about the abuse, I continued to suffer in silence for years and years. Never once did she ask how I was doing. Not once did she seek to get me into counseling or a program to help me deal with the abuse. Oh no, we would not dare let anyone know what was going on in our perfect residence on Fisher Street. That would have interfered too much with her grand masquerade. She refused to get me what I needed so she would have what she desired.

One day not long ago, I was sorting through some old photographs of myself. A photo from my high school days moved me. In the photo my eyes held deep distress. The pain was so raw that it overwhelmed me all these years later. I had to turn away from the picture because I was getting lost in the depth of the anguish I saw in my own eyes. It was like looking into an infinity mirror: there seemed to be no end to the agony those young eyes carried. I got so caught up in looking at it that I didn't notice that my daughter had come up behind me and was looking at the image over my shoulder. After examining it, Alexandra asked if I'd had friends when I was in school. I told her, yes. I was really surprised by the question. I hadn't been homecoming queen, but doggone it, I did have friends.

I had to know why Alexandra asked that question. I wondered, did I look like a loser to her? A nerd? She told me it was because I looked lonely.

My daughter was only seven when she asked that question. If a seven-year-old child could look at a twenty-year-old photograph and see that I was in pain, how could it be that my mother, who lived with me day in and day out and knew me from day one, had not seen my pain or respond to it before, during, or after the abuse?

Where was my mother? Where in the hell was my mother? I needed her help, her protection, her reassurance, but she was nowhere to be found. She had left me, abandoned me to fend for myself in a jungle of uncertain emotional trauma, panic, and disgrace. While she lay in the bed making love to george in the same bad in which he abused me; I lay alone in my room mentally tormented, stressed, scared, stained. I was left to try to figure it all out on my own. Left to my own devices, I tried to decipher my situation as well as an eleven-year-old mind could.

While I was disintegrating, I saw that george and my mother were going on with their lives as if nothing had happened. My brother, Alex, went on living his life oblivious to the secret depth of our dysfunction. I was the only one who was stuck. So I must be the one with the problem. My mother and george went on with their marriage; they continued to work their same jobs, had their same friends, and maintained their false sense of respectability in our family and community. My development was arrested. While their life went on, I was the one sitting alone in my room with the lights turned off.

❧

I couldn't find my way out of the dark dungeon to which my mother and george had exiled me. I believed that george was the evil one, and he was. But it wasn't until I was an adult that I could clearly see that while the foundation of my malfunction was the abuse, my stagnation, helplessness and anxiety came from being held prisoner in my own house, locked up with the man who stole my innocence—and my mother, my own mother, was the warden. She had held the key. Instead of releasing me, she kept me incarcerated and pardoned george. I remained in a prison that I had no idea how to escape. And my mother was my captor.

This woman looked like my mother, sounded like my mother, but who the hell was she and what the hell was she thinking about? Not about me. She thought about finances: she told me that george had to move back into the home because it was too expensive to maintain two households. She thought about appearances, about what people would say: she swore me to secrecy. I was to tell no one, especially not Alex. She wanted to protect Alex from the truth and george from the penalty. She thought about her own needs but never once considered mine. No matter what justification she offered, the bottom line was that she wanted george there. His presence fulfilled her. And the craving she had for george and what she felt he gave her was more important to her than I was.

So my mother got what she wanted, that sorry excuse of a man. george got what he wanted—my innocence, his lust fulfilled and my mother. He didn't have to pay for his sins, my mother made sure of that. There were no consequences for the grievous atrocities that he perpetrated upon my young body. My mother told me I could call the police if I wanted to, but... then george would have to go to jail and the family would suffer from the loss of his income. Now I wouldn't want that to happen, would I?

As I dealt with the ramifications of the abuse in my adulthood, I think I was at times less angry about what happened to me and more angry that my mother let down the veil of perfection to reveal a woman who was not "Mother of the Year," but quite the opposite. My mother's being a flawed, broken, and emotionally irrational person was what I had trouble forgiving her for. I had tried so desperately to hold on to my idealized image of her that for a long time I had suppressed awareness of her role in my tortured upbringing. At that point in my life, I couldn't handle the truth. I had made her husband, george, the villain and enemy, overlooking for years the fact that my mother was also guilty, even more so because she was my mother.

Writing this book, allowing myself to revisit my childhood and feel the pain, the lonely isolation, the repulsion, the anger, the disgust, the wrath, the despair, is excruciating. I am afraid I will get lost in it and will not be able to return. I am afraid to allow myself to feel this staggering pain.

I am fighting frantically to live and to love without fear and desperation, the things that I have known for so long. Sometimes it feels as if I've come a long way, yet I still feel so far from my destination. I have been fighting all my life. Not to gain any great prize; just to be seen, just to have my pain, my struggle, acknowledged and attended to. Just to be loved. I never wanted much; I just didn't want to suffer, not anymore.

I was left to sit in a pile of george's shit. I was left to sit in a pile of my mother's shit. I sat in their shit for so long that I began to believe it was my shit. I was sitting there and was not allowed to move, so I started adding my shit to it and claimed the whole heap of shit as my own.

My own mother set me up for a setback. Remember, she was the type who would have nominated herself as Mother as the Year. She prided herself on her closeness to her kids, the sacrifices she made for us. She prided herself on being able not only to take care of us but also to rescue other children who were in need of nurturing. She did do a lot of great things for Alex and me. There were some good times in our young lives that I can remember. We had a swimming pool in our backyard every summer, and a swing set. We would play baseball, cook out, and go on fun fishing trips. She raised us in the church; heck, the church met in our living room. Because of my mom's welcome, all the neighborhood kids liked to hang out at our house.

These things make sorting out my memories terribly confusing. If she had been an overtly mean and cruel mother, I could better understand the choices she made. But she was abusive, though not in an obvious way. Her abuse was silent, yet deadly. While she was out signing autographs as Mother of the Year, saving needy neighborhood kids and family members from motherlessness, her own damned daughter was in her own damned house dying right before her own damned eyes and she never took the damned time to take notice of how the hell I was doing.

After george moved back in the house, she never once asked me if I was okay. She never even asked me how I felt. She didn't give a damn. It's hard for me to admit, acknowledge and write these bitter words, but the truth is if she had of cared, she would have asked and she would have done something about it. If she "knew" my feelings, they would only have messed up her plan to keep the bullshit production of the perfect family going.

When george moved back in, it hardly seems possible, but things got worse, much worse. I was plagued by a constant sense that george was watching me. I thought that perhaps I was paranoid, but I would later discover that he was stalking me in my own home. He was obsessed with me. I attempted to protect myself by repressing all strands of evidence of sexuality in my developing body, in order to keep his stalking at bay, yet nothing changed. His horrifying hunger for my young body was insatiable. There were nights that I would wake to find george masturbating over my bed. Sure, I told my mother. And I was sure that she would kick him out for good and be totally through with him. Nope. She allowed him to continue to live with us.

When I was nineteen and woke up in the middle of the night to find that george was hiding in my closet, masturbating as he watched me. It seems like that would have been enough. Nope. My mother finally kicked him out, but she wasn't willing to let him go. She remained ensnared with him. For many years after that she made attempts to reconcile with him. I lost respect for my mother. After all george had put me through, had put our family through, I could not conceive that she could ever want to be with him again. One night when I was about twenty-three, she was supposed to go out on a date with him. This was after his girlfriend came to our house to tell my mother that george was hers now and my mother had best leave him alone.

That night he stood her up. She came back home, bursting through the door with all the tragedy of an afternoon soap-opera drama queen. Before my eyes, my mother fell on the floor and began to cry uncontrollably, kicking her legs and pounding her fists on the ground. I looked at her in total amazement and utter disgust. I could not believe that was my mother on the ground, hollering and crying over george.

She desperately wanted to be with him. She would become furious when I told her that she should divorce him.

I was engaged during this time. In those crucial moments, when I needed my mother to be teaching me how to have a healthy relationship with a man, I was on the front row witnessing all of this insanity. Instead of providing wholesome guidance, my mother was programming me to accept shit from all future relationships. No wonder I stayed in the abusive relationship with my husband for so long. By the time I met him, my soul had already been programmed to believe that I was nothing. I thought I was lucky that a man even wanted me at all. Of course I was going to accept as much shit as he sent my way. I had become so used to being in shit that I could no longer smell the stench of it.

My mother wore a filter over her eyes that affirmed that she was a wonderful mother. Nothing was going to make her change her mind about that, not even her own unforgivable behaviors. My pain, hurt, and anger contradicted her self-perception. She did not want to see her failures reflected in my pain. It was easier to ignore my pain than to change her opinion of herself or alter her destructive behaviors.

She never told me she was sorry for how her choices had shattered my life. I tried and failed to get her to see the error of her ways, but she was too far gone to admit her wrong. Once she said impatiently, *"I get it. I get it. You will never forgive us for what we did to you. But stop hurting me over it."* When she said "us," you'll never forgive us; she was voicing what I already knew. She had aligned herself with george against me; it was "us" against me.

The pain of what I endured was agonizing, and it has remained sharp through the years. It could have been eased a little if my mother had recognized her part in it and said she was sorry. Instead, her failure to apologize has felt like her stabbing me in my back, twisting the knife and then pouring salt into the wound.

In the end, I was disappointed to the core that my mother was not who I'd thought she was. She was not who I needed her to be. Why didn't she save me? I kept hoping and wishing for the day to come, but it never did.

How could my own mother subject me to so much suffering? For years I asked myself this question over and over again until I almost lost my mind. I kept hoping for some logical answer, but there never was one. I hated her. God help me, I hated my mother for what she allowed. At the very same time, I loved her and wanted to heal whatever dysfunction she has passed on to me.

I have never had a protective family covering, never. My biological father was never there. My stepfather sexually abused me, and my mother allowed him to stay in the home even after she found out, even after he tried it again, and again. I have never felt safe. I have never felt deeply safe, not once since I was six, though Alex has tried his best to help. A brother can't be a father.

Once my mother told me that if george got saved, she would consider reuniting with him. I sat next to her stunned, as if someone had just stuck a stake in my heart. What do I matter to this woman? Do I matter to her at all? Why is george more important to my mother than I am? I wondered where her righteous indignation was. Her anger? Her motherly instincts? This man sexually ravished her baby girl for five long, torturous years. How can she stand to see him, talk to him, let alone under any circumstances consider reuniting with him?

If I allowed it, she would expose my children to george. I have had several fights with her over this. When Alexandra was younger, my mother would keep her for me some afternoons at her job. I explicitly told her that I did not want george around my child. You would think that I wouldn't have had to tell her this, right? Well, yet and still, she left my daughter with him on more than one occasion after I had unambiguously asked her not to. The thought of that man touching my daughter sent me into a state of rage. I was livid. I felt betrayed. And I would be damned if I was going to allow my mother to put my child in the same shit she put me in. Her response? *"Well, if you don't think that I am fit to watch her, then maybe you should find someone else."* I was willing to walk away and not look back in order to protect my baby. This is the point that I began to realize that I needed some distance between me and my mother, but I didn't know how. I was still too enmeshed with her.

Not long ago, she and I were driving to a meeting together. On the way, she told me that she wanted to invite george to our church's twenty-fifth anniversary celebration to honor him for helping to start the church in our home. Keep in mind that we had church on Sunday, but Monday through Saturday he violated me in that same sanctuary. In that same sanctuary, he asked me to suck his dick. And she asks me if I would mind if he was invited to the celebration. *"Because, after all,"* she reasoned, *"he did allow the church to be in our home."* He allowed the church in our home? The truth is george never had the power to allow a damn thing in our home, which is one of the reasons I believe he sought me out. I think he was angry that my mother controlled everything. I believe that he used me to get back at her. Pay back is a bitch, isn't it?

I made a vain attempt to reason my mother out of this insane request that she had made of me. I said, *"Mom, that's like asking a rape victim if she minds if her attacker came to a celebration with her to be honored."*

"Well, I know that you might not prefer it, but let me know what you think."

I lapsed into silence and simply stared out the window. It wasn't just that I could not stand to look at my mother, at that moment, and that I was trying my best to avoid cussing her out. I wanted to see what color the sky was in a world like this.

Then I turned back to my mother and let her know how her request sounded to me. I told her that I could not understand how she could want george to be honored in any way, shape, form, or fashion. After the years of violation, abuse, savage stalking, and desecration that he put me though, she wanted him to be celebrated. No unrighteous offense, no amount of scarring and emotional damage, nothing, *nothing* that I endured, made a damn bit of difference to my mother.

It totally went over her head. She refused to apologize for the request. She did muster up a haphazard apology if I was offended, but she doggedly insisted that there was nothing wrong with wanting to invite george to be honored at the celebration.

I was insulted, devastated and angry, but most of all I was sick and tired of being sick and tired of allowing this man into places of honor that he did not deserve. He was at my graduation, and at my wedding and at my daughter's christening, being honored as the devoted stepfather. I couldn't endure that bullshit anymore.

My mother continues to consider herself an expert on mothering. She frequently points out what I am doing wrong. She tells me what she did and how she did for her kids. As she talks, I wonder silently, Mom, don't you know that I was there and I know the real deal?

She rarely gives me a compliment on my mothering but is quick to give criticism. I know that I am a good mother to my kids. The pitiful thing is that I would love for my mother to tell me that I am a good mother, but how would she know?

One day at my house, she started crying, tears running down her face. You want to know why? Because I was beating the living daylights out of my kids? No. Because I wasn't feeding my kids? No. Because I had a pedophile living in my home abusing my daughter? No. She was crying because my daughter Alexandra was wearing my son Christian's pants. She accused me of dressing Christian better than I dressed Alexandra.

I am sitting there in utter amazement thinking to myself, *"Damn it mom, when in the hell did you develop such keen sensitivity? You never once put up your sensitivity antennas for me. Yet you could sit in my house and cry because my child is wearing her brother's pants? Give me a break. What do you think you could ever tell me about raising my kids, Mom? Take a long look at your own damn self in the mirror, Mom. You are so self-righteous, so damn judgmental of everyone around you. Yet you are standing in a pile of your own shit that is a mile high and you act like you are sitting upon a bed of fresh red roses."*

For far too long I was consumed with trying to right the wrong that my mother had done to me. I was so concerned with seeking her love, desperately seeking her restitution and frantically seeking her restoration, that I was allowing the life force to be drained out of me. While I was searching for something that I would never find, my own daughter and son were looking to me to give them what I was still looking for. I thought that I could not really give it to them until I got it from my mother.

I had been waiting all my life for my mother to give me permission to live better, to expect better, to be better. I had been waiting all my life for my mother to show me that I mattered more to her than george, more than money, more than public opinion: what people would say or think about her "perfect life" gone bad. I had been waiting all my life for my mother to protect me, stand up for me, free me from the pain and the shame. I had been waiting all my life for my mother to give me what she never had herself: a sense of worth. While my focus was fixed on my mother as my savior, I was closing myself off from ever getting better.

I had thought she was the vehicle through which I would finally get my worth. How painful it is to long for something that is rightfully yours. You can see it and almost taste it, yet it remains out of your reach. My mother killed me in so many ways by her actions and failures to act.

After prolonged and unnecessary suffering, and disappointment after disappointment, I finally realized that I would never get from my mother what I needed to heal and redeem myself. If I was ever going to receive my redemption, it was going to have to be by my actions and choices and by God's power. My mother cannot give me what she does not have. I can't wait any longer. I have to be free, I need to be free. Not just for myself, but for my own children.

So, I have painfully come to realize that while you can love someone, you need not be in a relationship with them. Sometimes for your own good, you need to be separated. I began to create some physical and emotional distance between my mother and myself. I could only do this after I finally acknowledged that she wasn't changing, that nothing I could say, no tears I could cry, nothing I had endured, would make a difference. The closer I stayed to her, the more opportunities I gave her to abuse and disappoint me. I had to realize this was the mother I had. I could not alter who she was; I had to accept her as herself and deal with it. My mother was dragging me down into a pit of despair, a point of no return. She was taking me to a place where dreams die and desperation thrives. I just couldn't do it any more.

I used to make excuses for my mother because of what she herself had suffered. But a friend once told me, *"Your mother has to accept responsibility for the way she handled the situation in her own life. She was an adult when she made those significant decisions. There is nothing you can do to change that, and there is no reason for you to feel you need to help bear this burden. So stop making excuses for her."* He told me, *"The more you try to see reasoning behind her actions, the more you are going to be confused by the 'why' question, because there was no reasoning."* I had been trying to save my mother and myself at the same time.

My friend was right: there is no excuse for what my mother put me through, even though she had been through it herself. As a matter of fact, I think that makes it worse, because she knew how her stepfather's sexual abuse and her mother's subsequent choices had damaged her own life. She should have done better by me.

I can't bear to think my mother consciously knew about george's abuse of me when it was going on, but there were clues. There had to be clues. She ignored them. The parallels to her childhood experiences were overwhelmingly similar. She should have prepared me like I have prepared my daughter and son. She should have told me that no one had a right to my body. She should have told me that she would protect me if anyone ever violated me. She should have told me that I should never keep secrets from her. If she had ever asked me, I would have told her.

Recently my brother, like the friend quoted above, could see that I was losing myself in attempting to save my mother. He counseled me that I could not save both her and myself. I had to choose. I chose myself, because in choosing to save myself, I also chose to save my own daughter and my son.

Given the similarity between my life story and my mother's, you can see that there has been a generational curse in my family. Like the recipe to Big Mama's Pound Cake, my grandmother passed down her dysfunction, unresolved issues, brokenness, heartache, shame and disappointment to my mother, and my mother passed it down to me, adding her own special touches to the mix. To this day, my mother, who is in her mid-sixties, still yearns for the love and acceptance of her mother. Like a little girl, she still cries and wonders why her mother could not love her. She is still so engrossed and absorbed, as always, in her own pain, that she doesn't even realize that I wonder the same thing. And I, almost forty, realized that if I didn't stop searching for the answer to an unanswerable question, forty years from now, my own daughter would be asking herself that question too.

It's not easy for me to accept that I could be like my mother in any way; I have worked far too hard to be the exact opposite of her. Yet in my frustrated, obsessive quest for her redemptive love, the anger and disappointment that consumed me caused all of the negative things she possessed that I hated to increase in me. I was giving all of my energy and power away to her. Its not that I was at all trying to be selfish; I honestly believed that I would never have what I needed to give my daughter if I could not be redeemed by my mother. This mindset and unhealthy emotional state caused me to hold back emotionally from Alexandra.

I looked at my grandmother, I looked at my mother and I saw myself. I hated what I saw, too. I vowed to myself and God that I would continue to struggle until I found the start of a new path of living differently from it all. I could see myself repeating the same mistakes with my own daughter with different actions and for different reasons but with the same destructive results.

Oh, I say it's not the same to pacify myself and to spare myself the ugly truth that I, too, carry the curse. I can hardly bare to face the truth that it's hard for me to express the love I feel for my daughter because I have a battle with myself every day, finding reason, after reason, after reason to hate myself. I don't want to live like that and I don't want to set up my daughter, either.

In the name of Jesus, the curse stops here!

If I don't deal with the influence the abuse and neglect had on me, I will pass it on to Alexandra and Christian, and they will pass it on to their own children, and so on and so on and so on. I have protected my kids at all costs from being victims of abuse. So why should they still have to suffer from the abuse that I endured? I refuse to allow my children any direct exposure to this insanity, and I must also protect them from its indirect effects. I'm no longer a child, a young innocent victim with no choices and no options. I am a grown-ass woman, and I now realize that I don't need my mother's sanction, permission, or restitution to live. The truth is, as much as all the stuff my mother put me through still hurts, I choose for it to no longer matter. Her approval, authorization, appreciation and admiration don't hold the key to anything for me anymore; the truth is that they never did.

I don't have to say, "Mother May I" anymore. I don't need her permission to be safe, to be happy, to be free. I have got to free myself from the grips of the despair of the life that I have lived. I've got to work through this shit, because I know what will happen if I don't!

Chapter Nine
Oh, Drama!

Drama!

Lie, shuck, jive,
Act like all is okay

We must keep our drama going,
Each and every day

Don't cry, dry your eyes, suck it up
Don't tell anyone what's true

Smile, laugh, play,
Our masquerade is counting on you...

I could not believe it when I came to the realization that I created drama in my life even when there was none. But, drama was what I knew. Chaos was what I felt most comfortable with.

Lilada Gee

We humans are creatures of habit. We get used to things being a certain way, and then we find comfort in the familiarity. It does not matter if the condition is good or bad; all that matters is that it is the same. The preference for staying in the same state of being can keep us locked into patterns which are actually destroying us. Instead of making the changes that will bring life, we cling to what has always been, no matter how crazy it may be, as if our very life depends on it.

I have heard it said that the adult children from dysfunctional homes grow up and re-create their childhood family dynamics in their own families. This doesn't really make sense to me; you would think if you hated some horrific experience in your family as you were growing up, you would rebel against it and be sure to avoid it in your own family. The theory is that we re-create our childhood family because we have a subconscious need to right the wrongs we endured. We set the stage, if you will, with all of the characters and props from our youth, believing we can work out the dysfunction and come up with a better plot and ending in our own family. This sounds crazy, I know, but who am I to argue with the experts?

I grew up in an extremely dramatic family. My family was so good at our drama, no one even knew that we were acting. The triggers varied, but there was constant unnecessary drama going on in our household. Verline and george argued constantly. I often felt like I was in the middle of a war zone. Their arguments could become very bitter as they yelled, screamed, and cussed, usually about money. There was always a power struggle between them; but there was no question, my mother wore the pants in our family.

In case you were wondering, yes, I joined in the drama, just like everyone else in my family. I became so entrenched in the façade that I actually started believing the hype myself. I just wanted a normal life. If I could not have "the real deal" at least I could pretend I had it. So pretend is what I did. Let me tell you, I could act my ass off. I acted like I had the best mother in the world, until I believed it myself. I acted like george was the greatest step-father that a fatherless girl could hope for. Hey, who needs the real thing when you can fake it, right? Every morning it was "Lights! Camera! Action!"

Starring as the perfect mother was Verline. Her character was a loving and doting mother who put her children first and would die before she would let anyone hurt them. She was also the director who called the behind-the-scenes shots. Her co-star was george; he played the role of the hardworking provider and wonderful husband who had swooped in to rescue Verline from the despair of single parenthood. His character loved his stepchildren as his own flesh and blood.

My older brother, Alex, played a supporting role to my character. He really didn't know what was going on, but he was on hand to help keep the production going. He had no idea why I needed him to be a lifeline, but he was just that for me. Without him I don't think I would have been able to endure all that I did. He was the good boy who always did the right thing. He was a great brother and son.

I played the role of the sacrificial lamb. My character didn't have many lines, but I was in most of the scenes. My role was to be there, but be quiet. I was great in my role. I knew all of my lines by memory. "Shhhhh!" is not too hard to remember, is it?

What the audience didn't know was that behind the scenes the well acted and orchestrated "perfect" little family drama was a true nightmare. Verline, the perfect mother who lived for her children, in reality was willing to sacrifice me to maintain her image of the perfect life to the world around her. george, the model husband and stepfather, cheated on his wife with her own six-year-old daughter. The director, my mother, directed us all to continue to play our roles as if everything was fine in our perfect little world.

But the deception was eating me alive. I had begun to explore a personal relationship with Christ. I was still young, maybe nine or ten, but I knew that I wanted the joy and peace that my grandmother used to tell us Christ would bring into our lives if we lived for him. My grandmother was a sanctified minister, so naturally she also told us about hell. I can still smell the fire and brimstone from the stories that she used to tell. I did not want anything to do with the hell that she described. I figured I already knew what hell was and I had had enough of it; I wasn't about to spend an eternity in it too.

Looking back, I wish that I had had the strength to scream out. When george first started abusing me, I wish I had had the strength to try to protect myself, instead of him, my mother and Alex. I was my last concern. Everyone else had more value than I did. How does a six-year-old come to that conclusion? Well, I didn't come to that conclusion alone. george used emotional manipulation on me big time. He took advantage of the pure love that I had for him, my mother, and Alex. I did not have any love left for myself.

Day by day I went on acting as my script dictated, as if everything was fine. I have never considered myself particularly dramatic, though many of my friends would vehemently disagree. But I must admit that I must have been one hell of an actress to pull off this role. For five years I stayed in character, never once missing my mark or forgetting one of my lines. It was only late at night when I was alone in my dressing room that I'd let my true emotions out. Many nights I cried myself to sleep hoping that God, Elvis, Diana Ross and the Supremes or somebody would come and end this drama from hell.

As I continued to seek a relationship with God, I learned that what george was doing to me was against God's law. As my love for God grew and I began to feel his love toward me, I didn't want to be involved in anything that would jeopardize that for me. It was in that light that I finally gained the strength to finally open my mouth.

It was my convictions that finally gave me the strength to tell my mother the truth. I was afraid to tell; I thought that my whole life would come crashing down around me. But I knew I had to do it. I wanted to move forward in my relationship with God, and I knew that the ongoing abuse would not allow me to do so. I knew that I could not be an adulterer and serve god.

I had finally done what I'd thought I could not do, and it did not turn out the way I'd feared it would.

Initially, my mother seemed to respond in all the right ways. Thank God, I thought, that my mother believes me. As she consoled me and kicked him out of the house, finally I was going to be free from all of this crazy drama!

I couldn't believe how well it had gone. I had expected a lighting bolt to come out of the sky and strike me down. I thought learning of her husband's transgressions would kill my mother, but it didn't. She had come to my rescue and protected me. Life was good—or so I thought.

❦

Just as soon as I thought the dramatic production had shut down, we went back into production. This time we had an even bigger budget. We were able to expand the original script and add some new elements, including special effects. Like the little girl in the movie Poltergeist, I looked at the screen of my life and said, "He's baaaaack!"

One day my mother called me into the kitchen and sat me down. I thought we were going to have a nice little mother-daughter conversation. I thought that she was going to check in on me, you know, ask me how I was doing; make sure that I was okay and all. It turned out that production costs had gone over budget. My mother said george was going to come back into the house. The family had been suffering financially as he and she tried to maintain two households. But she assured me that he would never try anything with me again. She promised to protect me.

My mother, the director, stepped up the drama a few notches. I was not to tell my brother of the abuse. It would be too devastating for him, she told me. I was also directed not to tell anyone else, especially not my grandmother.

My mom tried to explain that george was not a bad person; he did what he did because he was sick and needed help. She opened up a college textbook and read to me from the text, which by the way was way over my eleven year old head. She wanted to illustrate that it wasn't about me at all; he was just using me as a replacement for her. Well and good, but she didn't bother to make sure that he got the help that he needed before she gave him access to me again.

She went on to explain that I could report his crimes to the police if I wanted to, but then george would go to jail. The family would not longer have his income and that would impact us all. "Did I want that?" she asked me.

My trusting eyes that began the conversation engaged with my mother's, slowly drifted away. I could no longer listen to her ridiculous words of betrayal and look at her at the same time. I figured that at least if I looked away, I could allow myself to pretend that this wasn't my own mother saying this foolishness to me. Yes, I was still just an eleven year old kid, but even I knew what my mother was saying to me was bullshit. But what could I do?

I thought the saying went "Don't do the crime if you can't do the time." Why did I have to decide? Why did she put the weight of that decision on my little shoulders? Why didn't she fully come to my rescue and save me, protect me, and demand that I get justice for what that sick, perverted man had done to me, her baby? I had believed the role that she played, her promise that she would protect me with her own life. But it was all an act. In the end she sacrificed me to protect her life, her image, her husband and the façade that she so carefully constructed. She could have stopped the madness, but instead she endorsed it, condoned it and added her own insane twist to it.

I thought to myself, Well, I'll be damned! And you know what? I was! My mother's decision to bring that man back into our home destroyed my life.

By the way, in case it hasn't been clear, my mother was a Christian throughout all of this. If she didn't know better as a mother, she should have known better as a woman of God: she should have known that what she was doing to her child was a massive violation of God's righteousness. But hey, we had a production to complete, right? All for one and one for all!

Just as I had begun feeling peaceful and safe, I was called upon to resume my role as the silent sufferer. I had hoped that when I mustered up the strength to do the right thing, my life would improve. It actually got worse. I'd thought that I was dead when all the abuse was going on, but when george came back into our home, I really died.

My family was so busy playing "perfect family" that I could not express the anger I had toward my mother's husband and toward my mother. I had no outlet, so I kept all of my fury on the inside and it was demolishing my soul, like a wild out of control tornado. Nothing escaped its destruction. I could not express my dark secrets to anyone in the outside world; I was sworn to secrecy. I could not be the one who would bring down the façade of our "perfect family." I had to hold everything together at all costs. It's a miracle that I didn't lose my mind in all of this craziness. Maybe I did.

If I had thought that my family had been a living hell before, my Lord, it was ten times worse when george came back! They were "back together," but my mom acted like she hated him. That still didn't stop her from reconciling with him! There was constant animosity in the air. The fighting, fussing, and cussing escalated. It was awful. The worst part was that I felt I was to blame for the intensified insanity. Yet we still kept up the pretense of the "perfect family" before the outside world. Damn, we were good!

He had to think I was fair game since my mother, knowing all, still renewed his contract and wrote him back in the script. No wonder he tried to molest me again and again and again after she welcomed him back in our home. He was a pervert, as you know, and perverts do perverted things. Why should he not? He had to believe he could have his cake and eat it too, especially after she refused to kick him out again after that.

She made some vain gestures, perhaps to ease her conscious that she was actually doing something on my behalf; but she didn't protect me. She made some empty threats that if he ever tried it again, she would tell his mother, coworkers, and friends that, as she put it, "he was a sick bastard."

Now I'm no network executive, but if she knew that he was a sick bastard, why did she let him back in the house in the first place? Inquiring minds want to know. But now we know she wasn't really about to mess up her "good thing" and tell anybody what she was endorsing in her own home, was she? His secrets were safe, her lifestyle was secure, I was neither.

Verline and george continued in their insane drama. As a child my choices were very limited. I had to live with them, but I tell you I was through with george fucking with me. After I released my secret suffering, I absolutely refused to ever allow him to ever touch me sexually again. I did that with the strength of God, no help from my mother. God gave me the strength to protect myself.

Believe it or not, growing up in that crazy house did not utterly destroy me—or so I thought. Since I was still walking, talking, and breathing, I assumed that I must be all right. I resumed life and lived it as if nothing out of the ordinary had ever happened. That was what was expected of me, and I aimed to please.

My life was kind of like an intense scene from the movie *The Prince of Tides* with Nick Nolte and Barbara Streisand. A pair of escaped convicts attack a family while the father is out at work. The convicts rape the mother, the daughter, and the younger son. The older brother comes to the rescue with his shotgun and kills both of the men. The mother makes the younger two kids clean up the bloody mess, while she has the older boy get rid of the bodies. She instructs the kids that they cannot tell their father; they are to act as if nothing happened.

The dad comes home, and everyone is sitting at the dinner table as if they are eating a wonderful Thanksgiving dinner. All except for the little girl. She can't fully pull off the staged show. She has put her pretty dress on inside out, backwards and over another outfit. Half of her head is in rollers, the other half not, and she is looking like she is a few eggs short of a dozen. No one says a word. She ends up being the family member who loses her mind overtly because she could not live the lie.

Like that family, after george returned we all lived as if nothing had happened. We went on family vacations, all staying in the same hotel room together, which by the way was shaming and shameful. We went to church in the livingroom and ate big Sunday family dinners.

I continued on with school, graduated and went to college. I was hoping to have a brand new start to my life. That's where I met Duane, the man of my dreams, who would become my husband. He was going to rescue me from all of this craziness and into the sunset we would ride and live happily ever after...

Chapter Ten
Loving You is Wrong, but I Don't Want to Be Right!

"You bitch!"

The power of his words knocked the wind out of me. It felt as if I'd just been hit in the stomach full force with a baseball bat. The cruel words burned through my ears, ran down through my heart directly to my soul.

Attempting to regain my composure, I struggled to believe the words that had just come out of my husband's mouth. I looked into his face; it was distorted through my eyes that were filled with tears. I was searching for a trace of the love I desperately needed. All I saw was anger and rage: he glared at me as if he hated me.

Duane ranted and raved like a maniac. His anger that night, as on too many other nights, was out of control. Here I was again at a place that I no longer wanted to be and had foolishly convinced myself I would never be again. Again, I was terrified, afraid of what he might do to me. Again, I thought he was going to hurt me. Again, to protect myself, I locked myself in the bathroom and again I called Alex to come over to help.

Two-seven-seven-four-four-three——. The tone of the buttons are deafening in my ears as I dial each number. My heart is beating violently, like the fierce, rhythmic, beats of the slaves' drums. My heart is pounding out a secret message, the desperate rhythm of a cry for freedom.

It seems like an eternity before the phone begins to ring. My heart beats faster with each ring, afraid that no one will answer; then what will I do?

"Hello?" the sound of his voice gives me the relief to finally cry. Up until that point I have been too angry and too afraid to cry. Silent tears begin to stream from my eyes, down my face and drip from my chin. "Hello?" I couldn't speak.

I am locked in my tiny bathroom in our apartment on Division Street. I am sitting on the closed toilet with my feet propped up on the bathtub. I have the phone clutched in one hand and a wad of toilet paper in the other; with which I try to catch the floodgate of tears now streaming down my face like a river. It's dark, one of the bulbs is blown out in the light fixture; it's late, I'm tired, I'm weary and I am worn. "Hello, Is anyone there?"

I wondered, is anyone here anymore? I lean over the sink and peer at myself in the medicine cabinet mirror. My eyes are red and swollen from crying, my hair is all over my head. I felt ridiculous, and I looked the part. I was looking wild and crazy; like a banshee that just got off of her midnight rounds.

"Hello? Lil, is that you?" Again I attempt to speak, but I still can't. The words get caught in my throat as I try to speak them. Only a desperate wail escapes from the pit of my belly; but in that wail was the story of my entire life. I was drowning in a jumble of emotions. I felt sad. Angry. Empty. Prideless. Lifeless. "Lil, what's the matter?"

I loved Duane until I could not love him anymore. I loved him until I no longer could distinguish right from wrong. I loved him until I could no longer think straight. I loved him until I lost myself. I loved him until I could no longer see clearly. I loved him until I could no longer feel the pain that he caused me. I loved him until what I felt no longer even resembled love. I loved him until my love for him slowly, painfully turned into hate.

It's not like love hurting was a surprise to me. It wasn't even a disappointment. Love hurting was what I knew, what I expected, what I sought. Love hurting was what I created for myself. It's what I needed, and felt comfortable with because it was what I thought I deserved.

Was I aware of the depth of my dysfunction? No. My subconscious mind was much too kind, or should I say cruel, to ever let me know just how far from sanity I really was. Besides, my mind recognized that if I had become conscious of how crazy my life was and realized I knew that I knew, I just might try to change some things. It couldn't have any of that. It wanted things to stay just as they were. So I kept on loving him, because I was sure that I was going to die if I ever stopped.

I knew that now we had reached the point of no return, but desperation and fear caused me to still continue to hold on. I refused to believe that all of my hopes for our relationship were dead. Anxiety gripped me; if Duane couldn't love me with everything I gave to him, who would? I needed love, even if it was painful love, tainted love, or not really love at all. Anything was better than nothing.

Duane and I met as students at the University of Wisconsin-Madison. When I met him I thought he was attractive. He had the big-eyed, puppy-dog look of a young man who needed someone to take care of him. That neediness drew me in; perhaps I thought it would give me an excuse not to have to deal with my own shit, if I had someone else's to concentrate on. We became really good friends. Our friendship swiftly evolved into a romantic relationship.

Duane and I began to date, and way too soon, we became engaged. Duane was sweet and kind; he loved the Lord and he was fine. He was everything that I thought I ever wanted in a man. By all appearances I had hit the jackpot!

Duane came into my life in the middle of my ongoing family drama. He fit into the production so well; it was as if he had a copy of the script. I thought he was playing the role of a dashing knight in shining amour that had come to rescue me, the damsel in distress. That's how he began, but in the middle of the drama, his character showed his dastardly evil side.

Duane seemed like one of the nicest guys you could ever hope to meet. Everyone liked him! He was constantly enveloped in a roar of laughter, making everyone around him laugh, too. But behind closed doors, he was a totally different person. Now ladies, I would be doing you a disservice if I pretended that there had not been a thousand signs of Duane's true nature before we got married. There were, but I decided to marry him anyway.

I was feeling worthless, good-for-nothing, inferior, mediocre, defective, flawed, and imperfect. I felt incapable, incompetent, unqualified, useless, sad, and plain old sorry. I couldn't believe that someone like him could really love someone like me. I wanted him. I needed him to be who I wanted him to be. He was going to redeem me.

I believed that Duane was going to ease all my aches and pains. Once I got him, I was willing to endure almost anything to keep him. I was certain that he was just the handyman that I required to repair my broken heart. I wanted him and I was going to have him come hell or high water. Well, both came.

The problems that I saw before Duane and I married should have been red flags. Instead, I saw them as a green light to keep going full speed ahead. I felt that I could encourage them away, pray them away, fast them away, love them away. Folks tried to tell me that Duane was not right for me. They don't know what they were talking about, I thought. I had already sized Duane up and had come to the conclusion that he was just what I needed to make everything wrong with me right.

I permitted my unexamined, unchallenged and unhealthy emotions to guide me instead of my common sense and spiritual discernment. You know how we women sometimes are. Before our emotions get tangled up in a relationship, we put together a long list of wants, needs, and demands for the man we desire to have in our lives. We actually even get a little indignant about all of the qualities we crave. But, when a flesh-and-blood man with a six-pack, bulging biceps, bow legs and a tight ass comes and starts whispering sweet nothings in our ear, we tear our list of desires into tiny little pieces. Things we'd swore we would never accept from a man we now think are cute.

Duane had awakened the sexuality I had worked hard to suppress for so many years. He and I got into some precarious sexual situations before we got married. He didn't make a home run, but he was definitely up to bat. So now I had my heart and my vagina talking to me. People tried to tell me that we were too young, that Duane wasn't ready to provide for me, that we should wait awhile before getting married. I was sure that everyone else was wrong about Duane and me, except for the two of us, that is my vagina and me.

One thing I now know for sure is this: two hurting people should not marry each other. This sets the stage for high drama! When I chose to be with Duane, I believed that if a man could feel my pain, we could understand one another and help one another through. This almost never works. One partner's pain usually outweighs the other's pain—or at least they think it does—and there the drama really begins! The thing that initially attracted us, now drives us apart. Our pain gets the better of us. The truth of the matter is that hurt people, hurt people.

Pain is no respecter of persons. It hits us all, the good, the bad, and the ugly, in every shape, size, and form. I believe that pain distorts a person's true character. So even when someone you would consider a "good" person meets pain, watch out! And as for those who already had serious character flaws—Lord have mercy, you're talking about a mess!

When Duane and I began to get serious, I had no idea of the magnitude of wreckage that the sexual abuse of my past had left on my soul. One of its impacts was that I had become very introverted. The secret shame I carried around made it very difficult for me to become involved in relationships with men. There were guys I liked, and a few I had brief encounters with, but Duane was my first real boyfriend. I was living in denial about the impact the abuse had had on me, but its devastating impact was undeniable. At the age of twenty-one, I was having my first real boyfriend. I believed I'd better hold on to him, because maybe the opportunity would not come around again anytime soon.

During our courtship, we had many difficulties. Generally I was crying more than I was laughing because of something that Duane said or did that wounded me. We had more than our share of arguments. Still, things weren't all bad all of the time. We did have some fun times. They were just too far and too in between. Sandwiched amid so much degradation and misery, they were lost. We broke up a few times, but quickly got together again. Because of our chaotic relationship, Duane and I were engaged for at least four years. That should have told us both something. It did, but I wasn't trying to listen. I was bound and determined that we could make it.

Finally we did it: we were married June 1, 1991. It was a spectacular ceremony. I was dressed in a beautiful white laced gown embellished with sequins, with a full length train. My head was crowned with a delicate veil that made me look like a princess. Duane was strikingly handsome in his all white tuxedo. We looked like a match made in heaven.

Our wedding was the talk of the town. I had 12, yes, 12 bridesmaids dressed in stunning red and silver satin dresses. We had all the trimmings, including a wedding cake that actually tasted good. It was my dream come true.

Duane cried like a baby throughout the ceremony. All the women present thought I was the luckiest woman in the world to have a man so happy to marry me. Yeah, that's what I thought. If I had known what lie ahead for me, I would have cried a bit more that day, too.

We had a wonderful honeymoon in Negril, Jamaica. I could not ask for more. I felt like my life was finally redeemed. Boy was I glad that Fear had convinced me to hold on. What was I thinking when I thought about walking away from all of this? Before it was all over, I was wishing that I had run away. Way too soon, the honeymoon was figuratively and literally o-v-e-r. In spite of having been sexually abused, I was still physically a virgin when we married; but emotionally and spiritually I felt like a whore. Maintaining my virginity was both a blessing and a curse. The blessing is easy to see; what I didn't anticipate was the curse. The last time I had had any type of sexual interaction, it was abusive—do you see where I am going with this? Not surprisingly, I had deep intimacy issues. Yeah, Duane had aroused my sexual desire, so I imagined that I was going to do okay in the sex department when we got married. I came to understand that being horny and being intimate are two entirely different things. A woman in my situation could progress through the intimacy issues in partnership with a loving, giving, and caring man. Duane wasn't like that.

"Hello? Lil, tell me what's going on?" I finally mustered the strength to open my mouth. After a long pause, I was able to talk to him, although it was English, he could barely understand what I was saying through all of the weeping. "Alex, can you please come over. I'm scared. Duane is going off and I don't know what he is going to do. I'm locked in the bathroom right now." I called Alex, as I often did during one of our blow-ups. This one was really bad, one of the worst. I was truly afraid of what Duane's next move was going to be. He was out of control. I felt such a sense of relief when I got Alex on the phone. He knew that I was in trouble, and as he always would, he came to the rescue.

Alex got to our house so fast I could hardly believe it. He had to be speeding all the way across town to our apartment. And when he arrived, he was ready to take care of business. He came with his infamous Jamaican walking stick. This was a former tree branch, thick, with detailed wood carvings of faces of nameless men engraved into every side. Well, one of those nameless men was about to taste a piece of Duane's ass that night.

Lilada Gee

As usual, Alex got us both to calm down. And as usual, we kissed and made up. And as usual, I told myself that things would get better, this time. And as usual, the vicious cycle started all over again.

Many relatives and friends who knew us as a couple thought that I was just the worst bitch. They would never see how Duane was treating me behind closed doors; they just saw the residuals of the impact. Just before we went into my brother's house for a family dinner, Duane would say something foul to me. As we entered the house, though, he would want to hug on me or hold my hand like we were on the Love Boat. It's not that he was repentant for what he had just said or done, he just wanted things to look a certain way to others. So naturally, offended, I would pull away, still be upset and hurt by what he had just said to me. He ended up looking like the one-armed teddy bear, while I looked like the bratty little girl who put it in the box for Goodwill. He played the victim role so well, but he was really the victimizer. There were times I was too emotionally exhausted to fight, so I would just go along with the drama and fake like all was well.

Appearances were everything to him. Everyday it was "Lights! Camera! Action!" We were the cutest couple. In public all was well; we would laugh, talk, hold hands, and coo at each other. We tried to never disappoint our audience. But when the director yelled, "Cut!" it was pure pandemonium. Part of the reason I stayed with him was I wanted to save him, more than I wanted to save myself. I wanted to make him happy, more than I wanted to be happy myself. My childhood had prepared me to mask and bury my feelings, because after all I was not important. What I endured didn't matter. At all costs, I must keep up appearances and, for God's sake, keep the family together.

I have to admit it though; Duane and I made the perfect couple. We both fulfilled one another's needs. He needed to shit on someone; I needed to be shit on. Without me around, who did he have to shit on, without him around, who did I have to shit on me?

One night Duane and I had an argument over something insignificant. I can't even remember what it was about. He wanted to take my car to go somewhere. (When things were good between us, it was our car. When there was trouble between us, I was always sure to remind him that it was my car.) I had taken possession of his key ring—a key ring I had bought for him, mind you. In his struggle to get them out of my hands, the key ring broke. He angrily threw the keys at the wall, causing a large hole over the livingroom couch. In retaliation he broke my favorite dresser-top mirror, one I had received as a gift. He became belligerent; but this was nothing new. It was more the rule than the exception.

Duane fussed and cussed all the time about everything; it was just like home for me. His fussing, cussing, and constant complaining escalated to verbal and emotional abuse. I worried that his mistreatment of me would spiral into a full-blown physically abusive relationship. There was an incident during one of our countless arguments that I can vividly recall. He and I were going back and forth with our heated verbal exchanges; then—out of no where—he punched me in my arm like he was Joe Frazier in the boxing ring with Muhammad Ali. Though that was an isolated event, there were many more episodes when the atmosphere that he created often caused me to fear for my physical safety. At those times, I was afraid of what he would do to me. In order to protect myself I would stay up all night, lock myself in the bathroom, or flee the house. When someone is physically abusive, the bruises are much harder to hide. But, when someone beats you down verbally and emotionally, only you truly know how deeply the wounds go. The verbal and emotional abuse worked out pretty well for me. My ability to hide my deep wounds allowed me to continue to live the drama.

It was pure hell, and I thought I was married to the devil himself. I suppose the drama in my marriage was so distressing because I had been sure that marriage to Duane was my one-way out redemption ticket from my destructive childhood.

Our marriage went from the sublime to the ridiculous. All the time, I was trying to make him happy—if I did this more, did that less, I hoped maybe we could have peace. He would yell at me because there was no food in the house, so I'd go shopping; then he would yell at me because he thought I had bought too much food.

He would yell at me because I didn't wash enough. So I would come home from work (while he was home all day playing baseball on Sega) and do the washing and put the clothes away in the dresser. He would come behind me and pull out his clothes and he would yell at me for not folding his T-shirts the right way. Nothing I did was ever good enough for him; nothing I did ever appeased him. But that still didn't stop me from trying. I kept trying harder and harder.

It was like living on a minefield. I never knew what was going to set him off. I tried to walk carefully, not to ignite him—but it didn't matter, he would always find a reason. Once when I was talking to Duane about getting a full-time job to help support the family, he went off. During our entire married life he had never had one. He threatened to "knock me out" if I said another word to him.

Okay, so I'm telling you all this crazy shit that he did. You must then be wondering why I stayed. Didn't I have better sense? Didn't I know that I shouldn't be treated that way? I had told Duane many times that the love I once had for him was being eaten alive by his rage and the bitterness and pain he was causing me.

So why did I stay? I was still under the false assumption that a man, good, bad, or otherwise, would ease all my woes. When I got mine, I was willing to do almost anything to keep him. I have seen many a woman in a high-drama relationship. As an outsider, I would wonder, Why does she stay? She doesn't deserve to be hit, misused, humiliated, hurt, and treated like that. I would wear myself out trying to understand, to no avail. I couldn't see that same crazy shit in my own relationship. I saw Duane as my lifeline, and I hung on as if my life depended on him. I refused to leave.

So why did I stay? Didn't I know the way that Duane was treating me was wrong? Abusive? On one level, yes, but remember: fathers teach their daughters how they are to be treated. Remember the six-year-old? Remember the lessons she learned? She learned to keep the family together no matter what, she learned to keep secrets, she learned that people who love you hurt you, she learned that her feelings did not matter, she learned to be invisible. She put all of the lessons that she learned into practice when she grew up.

So why did I stay? The pain I was in did not matter; I had to do what I needed to do to "heal" Duane, to make him happy. If he wasn't happy, it was my fault, and I needed to figure out what I could do to fix the situation. I actually convinced myself that I was doing the will of God in submitting myself to the abuse.

So why did I stay? I hadn't been abused enough, broken enough, hurt enough, disappointed enough, shamed enough, humiliated enough ...I stayed because, as bad as it was, I hadn't had enough.

During my pregnancy with Alexandra, Duane was downright cruel. He would not do a thing to help me. He would yell at me, cuss at me, throw things at me; he would drive like a madman if he got angry when we were in the car.

After Alexandra was born, things got better for a little while. Duane was a little kinder, a little gentler, and he loved his baby girl. We had a wonderful distraction. I thought, Maybe this was just the thing we needed. Alexandra gave me a renewed sense of purpose, drive and determination; I assumed she did the same for Duane. I assumed that she would be his inspiration for change. For a minute I assumed that things were really improving.

But it didn't last. The same abusive behavior soon emerged. Now I had to think about a victim other than myself: I had a little baby to protect.

For almost a year and a half, I took Alexandra to work with me. We could not afford childcare because I was the only one working full-time. I also was not emotionally ready to let my child be left in the care of strangers—I felt that if I kept her with me, I could protect her. So every day I would pack up her clothes, toys, and diapers and get her ready, take her to work,

work a full-time demanding job—and then come home to Duane, who had not gone to school again that day, again he had not done anything all day but play Sega. All the same, he still expected me to come home, cook, clean, wash, and yes, make passionate love with him. And he did not express his expectations graciously. Do you understand why I wasn't in the mood? Then my resistance became the problem: I wasn't being a good enough wife; I wasn't taking care of the house or of him.

The results of the stress of my abusive and non-supportive husband, pre-existing physiological conditions and hormonal changes ushered me into a terrible bout of post-partum depression when Alexandra was about two months old. Alexandra's pediatrician referred me to a counselor who specialized in the field.

Duane would sit in the counselor's office all up on me, holding me like a lovingly devoted husband during my sessions. "Wow," my counselor would say. "I am so amazed at how supportive your husband is to you." He would smile and play the part like a pro. I wanted to yell out, nooooooooooooooooooooooooo! Its fake, its fake! He's crazy! He's not nice, he's not safe. He's killing me. Please help me! But I didn't. It was like Duane had a concealed gun nudged in my side forcing me to go along with his crazy act, forcing me to pretend that nothing was wrong. I was too ashamed to admit that I was in such a hellishly abusive marriage. Everyone expected better of me and better for me. That fit right in with Duane. Oh my, he is the master of deceit. The deception of the life that I was living ate away at me like a voracious cancer. The truth was I was too mortified to get the help I needed because then I would have to admit that my reality was diabolically different from what we presented. Instead of crying out for help, I settled for the façade and I acted right along with him.

Duane was shiftless, lazy and uninspired, yet he acted like he was an entrepreneur, the next Donald Trump in the making. He was always doing some kind of business venture instead of getting a J-O-B. He ended up taking money out of the house to fund his next get rich quick scheme.

He rarely brought any in.

He wanted me to believe the hype, and for a while, I really did try. But, after one disappointment and then another, I couldn't believe anymore. Then that became the reason for his anger. "You never believe in me, you never support me", he would rant. So I would try to believe again, and I wound up trying to work the business for him, while he was either on to his next venture, or another game of Sega. There I was, trying to make him into the man that his daddy should have made him.

Duane, like most emotionally abusive men, was insecure. This is one of the reasons that they abuse and attempt to control others. They build a false sense of self by standing on someone else's ass. His neediness is what initially attracted me to him, now it was sucking out every bit of life that was left in me. There was no amount of anything I could give to make him feel whole, and there was nothing he could or would give to make me feel whole either.

I was unrelenting in my role of the happy wife. I lied to myself and all those around me, not in word, but in deed. Of course I did not dare share my secret with anyone. I sucked it up, stuffed it in, and pretended that my real life was a figment of my imagination. That's what I knew to do.

Day by day, week by week, year by year, the very life drained out of me, until there was very little of me left. I had become an empty shell. My heart and soul were broken. I was miserable. But, I continued to fake the happy marriage.

I wish I could say that I faked it because I stubbornly loved my husband and above all else wanted my marriage to work. Maybe that's how it started out. But as time progressed, I faked it because I was paralyzed by the fear of being on my own, what people would think, the shame that a failed marriage would bring my family, the harm to my child. What could I do? In my mind I was trapped, so my behind wasn't about to go anywhere.

I was in the pit of despair. I was under constant stress and strain, but that's how I grew up, remember? So it was what I knew. Besides, God knows that I didn't want my daughter raised without her father. I did not want to play the role of the single mother. I'd rather play the role of the secretly suffering wife and mother. The thought of her being raised by a stepfather was unbearable—you know why!

It took years, but I at last could be honest with myself and with Duane. I didn't want to take care of Duane anymore. I didn't want to carry him on my back anymore. I didn't want to be his damn mother, anymore. I wanted to be his wife and I wanted a husband, not another child.

I had finally had enough. So, at last, I left. I couldn't take another minute of the insanity. Now that I was pregnant with Christian, I knew what I had to do. I had been faking it with Alexandra, but I knew that I couldn't fake it with a second child in the picture. To save my children, to save my life, I had to give up my marriage.

I want to be clear here that I am not advocating divorce. I believe in the sanctity of marriage as ordained by God. For years I tried to save my marriage, went to marriage counseling through the church, was counseled by respected individuals and couples, and spent time before God himself crying out for my marriage. I made no rash decisions, and I advise any woman who finds herself in a painful marriage to consider her options carefully and work hard to save the marriage, but not at all costs. God gets no pleasure and no glory in two people staying together, while they are killing one another and killing their children emotionally and spiritually. You must be able to realize when enough is enough.

I was tired. I was depressed. I was disappointed. In my heart of hearts, I still had hoped that Duane would step up his game after we separated: deal with his out of control anger and abusive ways, get a better job, strive to finish school, demonstrate that he not only wanted his family, but was willing and able to do what he needed to do to provide for us. But he refused to get a full-time grown-ass man's job. I had 15 year old students in my summer youth employment program that were making more money than my husband and father of my two children.

I was three months pregnant with Christian when we separated. I carried my baby boy with such sorrow. Throughout the months of my pregnancy, things got worse instead of better. I allowed Duane to continue to suck the life out of me. Even though we were separated, he still wanted me to provide for him, as I always had. He wanted me to pay the rent, electric bills and other household expenses, while he did nothing, absolutely nothing to help to support me and Alexandra. Yes, he still expected me to take care of him. That's pitiful isn't it, but you want to know what was more pitiful? I still did. I said I had had enough, but hadn't. Not yet.

Duane and I were separated for two years. During that time, my hopes were dashed that the shock of my leaving would prompt him to make the changes needed to save his family. Duane never got it; he couldn't understand why I could not come home. He felt like he was the victim.

I would allow Duane to call me and abuse me via AT&T. I would allow him to abuse me when we would get together in our attempts to reconcile our marriage. I would still listen and take it like I thought I deserved it. I didn't even realize that I could simply hang up the phone or leave. I had been thoroughly conditioned to be victimized. As hard as I was fighting for my life, the victim mentality, that I still allowed to dominate my mind, was fighting for deadly consistency.

There continued to be threatening and abusive encounters throughout our separation. But you won't be surprised to hear that we kept up the dramatic pretense anyway. We would sit by one another at church as if nothing had changed. It was months before people in my own family knew that we were separated. I kept it up until I couldn't take living a life of deception anymore. I opened my mouth and I told people.

As I started coming into truth, I began to stop allowing Duane to treat me any kind of way. I began to stop allowing him to call me or come by my house and be abusive in my new domain. I started exercising the choice that I had in the matter. When he would pick up the kids for a visit he would be rude and crude, so I stopped him from coming to my house. I can remember one incident when he accused me of having an affair and being pregnant by another man. Trust me; at that point in my life another dick was the last thing that I needed.

As I began to shield myself from his attacks, he increased his force. During one of his tirades, I asked him to leave my house, he refused. I attempted to close the door and he put his foot in so that I couldn't. He continued to attempt to force his way into my house. I was on the verge of obtaining a restraining order because he was getting more and more out of control. Still, he couldn't understand why I wouldn't come home.

Now I will readily admit that I was still stupid, but I wasn't crazy. Think about it. Life with him had been miserable. He continued to treat me like shit after we were separated. He left me with the full financial, emotional, and physical responsibility for our children. What was there to go back to? For a woman, the ultimate betrayal is for her man to relinquish responsibility for his children. How could I go back to a man that I had to sue in court in order to get him to take care of his own children by his own wife—not just some woman that is claiming that he is her baby's daddy, but his wife! His next game plan took him to an all-time low. He had the audacity to sue me for alimony. I provided for everything that Alexandra and Christian needed, while he gave nothing, even so, he wanted me to still take care of his trifling ass. When I refused to keep caring for him and actually required him to take care of himself and his children, he tried to literally take the food out of the mouths of his children.

The longer I stayed away, the more sure I became that I would die if I ever went back to him. Because I refused to go back home, he became more bitter, more angry and more cruel. He continued to attempt to emotionally manipulate me, but it no longer worked. I had begun to succeed in changing myself and my circumstances. Meanwhile, Duane not only remained the same, he got progressively worse. When he saw that I had changed and was no longer willing to live within the crazy cycle of dysfunction that we had both created, rather than trying to change himself, he accepted defeat and filed for divorce. Maybe he thought that was going to scare me into taking him back. It didn't.

My divorce from Duane was the best thing for my babies and me. And though some people try to tell me what I should have done, they didn't have to live my life, I did. I know beyond a shadow of a doubt that I am in God's will and I know that he made a way for me to escape a situation that was too much for me and my children to bear.

Even after the marriage ended, Duane tried to keep the drama going. He was a deadbeat dad for years. About a month after we divorced Duane moved two thousand miles away, changed his first name, and began to act like he was young and single and loved to mingle. Though he claimed, to all those who would listen, that all he wanted was his family and to be a part of his kids' lives, three years passed with him making only sporadic phone calls every then—more than now—and visiting the kids only once. This was devastating for Alexandra. During this time, he also lied and cheated to dodge making child support payments for two years. That is until it caught up with him. It took the threat of jail to make him do right by his children.

I will admit that from time to time, I would allow myself to get pulled into the drama. I would go dust off my old script, and Duane and I would resume our roles. Now you know this didn't make any sense. Why go through the trauma of divorce if I was going to continue the drama? I almost lost my life until finally I learned: it takes two to tango.

After all my efforts and prayers, God helped me to see that the life that I was living was neither of his making nor of his pleasure. I was not serving or honoring him by allowing myself and my children to be subjected to abuse. God helped me to see that I could not change Duane but I could change two things: myself and my circumstances. At any point, if I refused to get on stage, the dramatic production would have to stop. It was time for me step to off the high-drama stage, but I wasn't ready yet for the drama in my life to end. I would still have to undertake a long journey before I could be free...

You know, I was just about to end this chapter, but then I got to thinking. I've made it look as if I was a perfect little angel during all of this madness, haven't I? Okay, I'd better be honest. Our marriage became a cesspool of anger, bitterness, disappointment, and resentment. I became the bitch that Duane said I was.

Living every day in misery, I became miserable. I began to do and say things that I could not stand. Rage and resentment began to devour me, and I was permitting them to turn me into someone I was never meant to become.

I was extremely wounded, but instead of dealing with the pain I had brought into the marriage, I made Duane and his issues the reason that everything in my life was going wrong. Given his abusiveness, he did have more than his share of responsibility for our marital problems, but I must admit that I bore some responsibility too. I came into the marriage, just as he did, with a great mound of hurts, pains, and unresolved issues.

Unfulfilled desire leads to desperation. Desperate people will do desperate things. I was hurting more than I could put into words from Duane's devaluing of me. I had invested all of my hopes and dreams in him. I had been sure he was the remedy for everything that ailed me. Instead of getting better, though, I became much worse because of the abuse, much more desperate than I could stand being.

I began to fantasize about having an affair. Yes, I knew it was wrong, but I felt that my pain gave me the right to seek any tonic that I thought would alleviate it. I still foolishly believed all I needed was a good man to make everything wrong in my life right.

You never can be certain where desperation will lead you once you start down that dangerous road. You begin on the road thinking that it will lead you to where you really want to be. Before you know it, you are in Never-Never Land, doing all the things you swore you never ever would.

I began to justify my dangerous thoughts, opening the door to the black hole of self-destruction. I was a ticking time bomb, about to explode, but still I wasn't willing to let go. I looked in the mirror and was disgusted by the woman I had allowed myself to become. I was so busy trying to hold on to Duane that I was losing myself.

Chapter Eleven
Fear Factor

I feel it coming, slowly, surely. It starts gradually, almost going undetected, initially. It twists and turns around my body, inch by inch, tightening its grip on me as it spirals up my body. I can hear it hissing as it continues to ascend, wrapping its rough scaly body around my waist.

It becomes harder for me to breathe the tighter and tighter it clenches me in the death hold that it has on me. I gasp for air. My heart starts to beat rapidly, I now know what has begun, but I don't know how it is going to end.

It reaches my head and coils around it, totally engulfing my mind. Utter terror is what I feel; an anxiety attack is what I am experiencing. I quickly jump out of the bed; thinking if I move swiftly I can shake it off.

The darkness in my room that swayed me to sleep just hours before, now feels like it is enveloping me. I feel so vulnerable, alone, scared. I begin to pace my bedroom floor. Back and forth, I walk, hoping that I can persuade this unwanted visitor to leave quietly before anyone gets hurt.

Like a stalker, the feeling of doom that an anxiety attack brings, follows me into the shadows of my life, waiting for the perfect time and place to attack me while my guards are down and I am too weak to fight back.

You must be wondering by now, How in the world did this woman make it through all the madness that she endured? I ask myself that question all the time. Well, I got by with a little help from my friends. One in particular has been a very good friend. She has really been there for me. Without her I know that I would not have made it this far. She has been there by my side, through thick and thin. And you know what? She has never, ever let me down. She was always there when I needed her. No matter how early or how late it was, I could always count on her to be there. We had an unbreakable bond. You see, we grew up together. She instinctively knew when I needed her. She would always arrive on the scene just in the nick of time.

She was there with me all throughout school, she hung out with me and all my friends, she went to work with me, she spent lots and lots of time at home with my then—husband and me. And whenever I went out of town, I took always took her with me. We were the best of friends, totally inseparable.

How rude of me—I must have lost my manners. I forgot to introduce you to my friend. It is with great pleasure that I present to you my very best girlfriend. Her name is Fear.

For the greater part of my life, Fear ruled my every day and my every night. I lived my life according to the crippling dominion of Fear. I didn't dare make a move or any important decision without first consulting her. Fear became a god in my life, because I allowed her to have complete dominion over me. I believed that Fear was in my life to protect me from all the things around me that could harm me. If I was unsure of things, people, or experiences, I would allow

Fear to step in and take over for me. Fear was the type of friend who could finish my sentences; she always knew what I was thinking. We had it like that. Sometimes I would forget things that had happened, but Fear never did. She was always there to remind me of my past. She would tell me that I had been hurt and therefore I should not trust anyone but her.

Now that I have explained how close Fear and I were, you can understand why I was upset when a friend once told me that Fear is "False Evidence Appearing Real." I really did not get what he was saying. It was hard for me to grasp that definition because I had great respect and reverence for Fear. I mean, Fear and I had a history, we went way back. I have to admit that I actually was upset with him: he had insulted my friend Fear. I was like a child who had just been told that her imaginary friend is only a figment of her imagination. I thought to myself, How dare he say that Fear is not real?

You may be wondering how Fear and I became so well acquainted. I first met Fear when I was six years old. I didn't remember ever meeting her before. I had always been a carefree child who had a zest for life and wasn't afraid of anybody. The sparkle in my eyes led me from one adventure to another. So I was a little shy when I first met Fear. Fear wasn't at all familiar to me; she was different from all the friends I was used to playing with. But we met at a time when I really needed her.

There were many signs during my courtship with Duane that told me this was not the man for me. I saw the handwriting on the wall, I just refused to read it. He looked the part and for the most part acted the part—well, at least in public. He was enough of what I wanted in a man, so whether it was a conscious or subconscious decision, I decided to settle. Don't get me wrong; he had a lot going for him. He was fun loving and smart, he was saved and he had so much potential. I was sure that he was going places, and I wanted to be right there by his side when he arrived.

When we first starting dating, our relationship seemed to be everything I had ever hoped to have with a man. We really liked one another and enjoyed spending time together. We were constantly engulfed in laughter, and we shared a love for God. This, I thought, was the man I had been waiting for all of my life. I exhaled.

When things started going wrong, I couldn't clearly see it. Okay, let me stop trying to be cute and be honest: I could see it, but I refused to deal with the truth of my situation. I avoided looking at the obvious signs. I folded up the map and put it away and kept traveling down a path that I would later deeply regret.

When we were first dating and Duane would explode with anger toward me over the smallest matters, I pretended the outbursts did not happen. When I repeatedly let him use my car and he would return it on empty, I didn't tell him that he made me feel unappreciated. When he expected me to pay every time we went out, I didn't tell him that it made me feel used. I didn't have enough worth to demand more of him and expect more for myself. Why? Because I was afraid that I would lose him if I asked for too much.

During arguments he would call me names or swear at me, disrespect me, but I wasn't insulted enough to leave him. After some of our arguments I didn't want to go to sleep because I was terrified that he would hurt me as I slept, so I stayed up all night—but I still stayed. Though I was afraid of what he would do to me, I was more afraid of what I would do without him.

You may be wondering if any of my friends ever told me to leave him, if they ever warned me that he was not good for me. Yes, they did. I considered what they said, but then I realized that they did not know me or care for me as much as my longtime friend and companion Fear. So I decided to consult Fear about it. She would know what I should do. Fear and I sat down over a cup of coffee, and we had one of our heart-to-heart girlfriend talks. She told me, *"Yeah, I know that he is doing some crazy stuff, but girl, you know he is so fine."*

"I know," I replied, *"but Duane has really hurt me."*

"Yeah, sweetie, I know he has hurt you, disappointed you, dissatisfied you, disillusioned you, and displeased you, but he has so much potential. If you leave him now, some heffa is going to

benefit from all that he, maybe, sometime in the future, will be."

I said, *"I hear you, Fear, but it's gotten to the place that I am afraid of him; I don't know what he's going to do to me if I stay."*

"Okay, so he called you a bitch and he threatened you, but if you let him go, you may never find anyone else. You know that he has that good hair. You all are gonna have some pretty babies. The next guy that you find might be ugly, and you might have some ugly babies with nappy hair. You know you don't want that."

In the end, the voice of Fear always won out. I trusted her more than I trusted my aunt, who warned me that he was not for me. I trusted her more than I did the counsel of my brother and pastor, who felt we were not ready for marriage. I trusted her more than I trusted the small still voice inside of me that told me I deserved being treated better than Duane was treating me. As bad as things were between us, I was still too afraid to do something different.

I knew the way that I was living wasn't right; nevertheless, I was ultimately too afraid to walk away. I was too afraid of what people would say. I was too afraid that someone else would get him. I was too afraid to be alone. I was too afraid of being a single mother. I was too afraid of having a step-father over my daughter. So, I sacrificed myself and, for the sake of Fear, stayed with him. I had convinced myself that I could fix whatever was wrong with Duane that caused him to treat me as he did. I told myself that all he really needed was for me to show him real love. I could heal all the pains of his past and make everything right.

The truth of the matter was that I had not dealt with the hurts and pains of my own past, which is what in turn, led me into an abusive relationship in the first place. So there I was, supposedly in the name of the love of God, trying to fix him and love him right, and I was in need of as much fixing as he was, maybe more. I was in desperate need of self-love and self-worth, the kind that can be fueled only by the love of God. I had nothing to give.

As we moved into married life, the foundation for dysfunction had already been erected, fortified, and decorated. Both my husband and I brought the sins of our fathers and mothers into our relationship. Upon that foundation we began to carefully construct our own destructive lifestyle. In retrospect, I can clearly see that neither one of us was a bad person per se.

Lilada Gee

We were both extremely hurt people, with unresolved childhood issues that were permeating our adult lives.

At this point, we had gone too far to ever go back. He knew he could treat me wrong and I would still love him. Neither of us had any incentive to change. He seemed to be fulfilled by treating me any which way, and I was fulfilled in taking all the crap that I could stand from him. I thought this was what love was all about.

I had actually convinced myself that this was the mission God had for my life. I really believed that I was doing God's will. Anytime I began to get a whiff of the common sense that my mama should have given me, Fear came and whispered words of encouragement to make me believe that it was in my best interest to stay.

Fear. Oh yes, she seems like she is your friend, but she will lead you to live a life that is contrary to God's plan for you. Every thought, every decision, and every move you make will then be filtered through her cruel web of deception. Fear will lead you to live a life in which you will be both abused and abuse. Fear will cause you to lie, to steal, to cheat.

Fear will tell you to grab the first thing that looks like a man and marry him, because you are too afraid that nothing better will ever come along. Fear will persuade you to support a man financially, emotionally, and spiritually, because you are afraid he'll leave if you don't. She will actually convince you that you can't make it without him, when the truth is you are already doing everything yourself.

Fear. It doesn't take a lot to totally interrupt, disrupt and erupt your entire existence. Fear will have you stay with a man who is abusing you, because you are more afraid of being alone than of being abused. You may live a life that may look like the real deal, but it's a cheap imitation. I know, because I lived that fearful life.

Fear speaks with assurance and authority. She presents herself as an ally, an expert on any and every matter. Fear, the wise and the all knowing one. She lulls you into a false sense of security, masquerading herself as your very best friend, your greatest protector...but my dear sister, Fear is your greatest enemy.

Fear tells you it's too soon, it's too late, you're too fat, you're too skinny, you're too ugly, you're too pretty, you're too Black, you're too White, you're not educated enough, you're too educated. Fear is the opposite of every truth that God is trying to cultivate in your life.

Fear caused me to turn down the volume of the voice of God within me. Whenever God would speak, Fear ran interference so that I could not hear him. If by chance a word from God got through—perhaps through something that was said in a sermon—in my soul, I would want to move on that truth and implement it, yet I continued to allow Fear to immobilize me. Finally it had gotten so bad that I was afraid to live, because Fear had convinced me that living would kill me.

I needed Faith; it was the only thing that was going to bring me out of the mess that I had allowed Fear to create in my life. God's words bring life, so the words of Fear must bring death. The more that I listened to and lived by Fear, the more my truest self died.

As I began to listen to and digest the Word of God, however, it became a part of me and caused my Faith to increase. As Faith increases so does life. If Fear is indeed false evidence appearing real, then Faith is factual and inspirational truth and hope. In other words, Faith is the evidence of the true reality that we seek, but cannot yet see.

Faith had been there all along, it had just been silenced by Fear. When I finally got tired of how I was living, I began to recognize the voice of Faith within me.

Faith—she's my girl now. I had to let Fear go when I started hanging out with Faith. I have to admit that there were times that I missed Fear. We had gone through so much together. At first I wasn't sure that I could live without her. I had become so accustomed to being with Fear; I didn't know how to live not including her in every aspect of my life. But the more that I hung around with Faith, the less I missed Fear.

Faith inspires me to have the courage to walk, no, run away from destructive behaviors, decisions, and relationships. She helps me to know that even if the man I thought was for me is gone, I can hope for a better situation. She helps me to go for dreams, telling me that even if I fail, I can try again until I succeed.

With the help of my girl Faith, I began to believe that I could, should, and would live a better life. She helped me to come to the decision that I could do bad all by myself. I would rather be by myself than to continue to live a life of death with someone in the coffin beside me.

The journey from Fear to Faith was a very difficult one, but like all journeys, it began with one step. Faith gave me the courage to begin to believe that my life could be better than it was. I began to believe that there was hope for me.

Chapter Twelve
As Good As It Gets

This is one of those days. I lie in my bed, paralyzed. I can't move. I cannot move! I just want to shut down, shut out everything and everyone around me. Just staying alive is an everyday fight. Sometimes I feel like fighting, some days I don't. I want to give in to the darkness and have it totally envelop me. Why can't I be better? Why can't I do better? I can't believe I am feeling like this again. I have tried everything- prayer, positive mental attitude, affirmations, herbal teas, colonics—yet again and again I wake up to a morning like this one. I want to sink slowly and steadily into the despair that is all around me.

I feel like an inmate, chained and shackled, in my own body. I feel powerless to stop the downward spiral that began the moment I opened my eyes this morning. I tell myself, My kids deserve better than this. I should do better for them even if I can't or won't for myself. I sink deeper into my vast cavity of despair, because I cannot muster the strength today to do better even for my own babies.

As I was growing up, my life seemed as if it was going nowhere before it had a chance to begin. The raping of my young body and soul left me feeling hopeless and helpless. I could not image how I would ever overcome what had overcome me already. I began to experience life through the filter of depression. I was convinced that my feelings of worthlessness, sadness, and despair were a true reflection of my reality. I was often irritable and anxious. Anxiety made me more irritable, and irritability made me more anxious. I went from feeling hopeless and helpless to being hopeless and helpless.

I believed that God could save my soul, but I did not know that God could redeem my life. The place beyond where you believe God can reach you is a scary place to live. That place makes South Central L.A. seem like Mr. Rogers' neighborhood. Once I reached that dead end, I ceased living and went into survival mode. I did just enough to keep my head above water; that was all I had the strength and courage to do.

In retrospect, I realize that depression was nothing new for me. I had been plagued with childhood depression, beginning not long after my inauguration into the complex adult sexual world of my parents. As a little girl I exhibited the classic symptoms of depression. I was sad, restless, and anxious. I really struggled in school. I had difficulty concentrating and focusing on academics. My grades began to reflect this. Terribly shy, I withdrew from peers and group activities. I was often absent from school with psychosomatic illnesses, which I mostly believed were real. There were many days when I just could not handle the academic and social pressures of school. My mind was some place else. On such days I would have one of my infamous non-specific, I don't want to go to school today, stomachaches.

In second grade I was put in a special group for kids struggling in school. By the time I was in the fifth grade, I had missed so much school that I was assigned to special education classes. In front of my entire middle school, I was voted one of two kids who had missed the most school. I was humiliated.

The sad thing was that I was really an intelligent kid. I could have excelled in school. Instead, I floundered, which made me feel even worse about myself, which made me even more depressed. The sexual exploitation and emotional neglect that I endured left nothing in my life untouched and unaffected.

Depression started in the backseat of my life. Before I knew it, it had climbed into the front seat and had taken over control of the wheel. I relinquished myself to a power that I was convinced was too forceful for me to conquer.

❧

I hate trying to describe depression. People who have never encountered it will never understand. People who have had to endure it think that words can never do it justice.

Depression is somewhere between the worst part of life and the best part of death. It's a cold, dark, lonely, cruel state of being in which I cursed the day that my mother was conceived, let alone the day that I was.

Imagine if you will: I am minding my own business, living the best I know how. One day I wake up and find myself uprooted from everything, everyplace, and everybody that is familiar to me. I am in the middle of a dark, damp cave. I just find myself in this frightening place; I have no idea how I got there. I see no entrance to the cave, and I can see no exit. I don't know if there is any way out. I'm confused. I'm afraid. I'm alone.

I yell until my throat is too sore to emit another sound, but no one comes to my rescue. I am trapped in a place from which I can reach no one and no one can reach me. A foul, rank smell envelops me and strangles me as I struggle to take each breath. All around I hear the stealthy movements of hungry creatures, laying in wait for an opportunity to seize and devour me. I am debilitated by a vicious fear.

My numbed mind faces two choices, each of them equally dreadful. I can stay where I find myself and hope that whatever got me there will come back and get me, or I can try to get myself out of the middle of nowhere. I try to move, but I can't see anything in front of me. Each step is laborious as I struggle through murky waters full of sludge. I don't know if I am moving toward freedom or toward damnation. Panic grips my heart with each step I take. Will the next step be my last? I hope so.

When I am in the midst of an episode of depression, it doesn't matter what I have or who I'm with. It feels as if nothing and no one can reach me—not even God. Depression is a state of massive deception, distorting everything that is true about life and the world around you.

For me, the cruelest part of depression is that it's like living inside a glass dome. I see life all around me, but the glass separates me from it. I couldn't touch it or feel it even if I wanted to. I become a voyeur in my own life. I initially try to fight and break through the glass, unaware of how formidable an opponent I am up against. The harder I fight, the more tightly I am trapped. When I cannot fight any longer, I collapse, all strength drained out of me, giving up on the hope of survival, awaiting the imminent fate of consumption.

Depression made me go to bed wishing I wouldn't wake up in the morning, and it made me angry every day that I did. Those of us who have had to face this demon have tried all we know how to break free. To rid ourselves of this dreadful disease, we try to smoke it out, sex it out, educate it out, counsel it out, medicate it out, shop it out, snort it out, shit it out. In the end, we find that no matter how much we do, or who we do it with, no external effort alone conquers depression.

One of the most frustrating and devastating aspects of depression is that just when you believe you have finally survived its wreckage, and are willing to take another try at living again; you drop down into yet another pit of despair and the merciless cycle starts all over again.

I was terribly depressed, but I didn't know it. I thought it was just me. I thought that I was too damaged, too weak. People can overcome a lot of things in this life, but I could not imagine how

I could overcome being me. I did the research: I could change my nose and my eyes, and I could have my belly sucked out. I could remove blemishes, reduce the appearance of my pores, and increase the size of my breasts. I could even change my sex. But as much as I searched, I could never find any doctor who could do a soul transfer.

The more I fought against depression, the more I felt dominated by it. The most powerful thing that fed my depression was the way I was allowing myself to live. Depression wasn't my enemy, I was.

Once I realized that depression was going to be around for awhile, I Finally decided to befriend it. I know that sounds crazy, but Winston Churchill said, "Keep your friends close and your enemies even closer." When I befriended depression, I began listening to it and discovered that it had a message for me, a message that would save my life. My soul was calling out to me in an effort to reveal to me that the life I was living wasn't life at all. Depression was my soul's call for help, telling me that my life was way off track.

My soul had been trying to talk to me, but I hadn't been listening. I was ignoring the signs along the road I was traveling that warned the bridge was out and I needed to take a detour. No way! I was bound and determined to stay on the same road of pain, death, and destruction that my life had always been on, because that was as good as I thought it could ever get. I had become a willing victim, trapped by my own fears and resolved that things would never get better for me.

Depression was the only way my soul could get a message through to me. For me, depression was like the scene from the movie Exorcist when the possessed girl is trapped deep within as the demon has taken over her body. From within her own soul, she writes on her stomach, "Help me." Depression was a message from my authentic self, which was trapped deep within, crying out for me to set myself free.

For so long I was heavy laden with pain. My pain. Yes, it was my pain! I named it, I claimed it, I became it. I allowed it to take over my life. I allowed my pain to lock me into to a place of desolation for far too long—to keep me in a constant state of suffering, to keep me a victim, encouraging me to let misery flow into every area, aspect, and component of my life. I was so full with sorrow that it overflowed and affected all those around me. My pain was in control, consuming me. I was in chronic pain of the soul. I was in distress. I hurt so bad that all I could produce was pain—more pain for myself and pain for all those around me.

At some point I moved from trying to alleviate my pain to pacifying it, justifying my actions or non-actions based on my pain. It was my legitimate excuse for not living legitimately, not fully loving, not fully embracing who God had created me to be. I expected life to make space for my pain the way a big woman's thighs make space for her hips as they work their way into her teeny Daisy Duke shorts.

When Duane and I divorced, I took a lot of time to think about and be angry for all the things I thought he had done wrong. I was bitter. I wanted to roll around in my pain, bask in it, have my friends and family acknowledge and appease it. I wanted to give in and give up on life because I was a victim of sexual abuse and neglect. I decided to surrender my life to all the pain, disappointment, shattered dreams, and depression.

As long as I focused on Duane and what he did or did not do, I could not focus on the parts of my own life that I needed to work on. By then he was two thousand miles away, living his life, doing whatever the hell he wanted to do, but I was still wallowing in the pain that he left behind. Now that just doesn't make any sense at all, does it? It seemed to then.

As long as I focused on all the painful and crazy shit that my parents and Duane put me through, I would never be able to move beyond where I was—and where I was, was stuck.

"Don't blame the victim"—we hear this, we know this, and I don't mean to offend anyone who is currently, has been or will be a victim. I still am a card-carrying member of the VIP (Victims in Pain) Club, so don't get me wrong here, okay? I am not saying that I or anyone else—especially an innocent child—has done anything to deserve to be victimized by anyone. But, as an adult survivor of victimization, I didn't think I had any responsibility for how I was currently living. I didn't think I had anything to change. I expected everyone else to change and create the fantasy life that I desired, instead of living the real life that I had.

I kept waiting around, wanting those around me—george, my mother, Duane—to finally see the light and stop all of the madness. They never did. I finally had to ask myself, *At what point did I leave the role of victim and become a victimizer of myself by staying in situations which kept me victimized by others?*

To end the atrocious cycle of victimization, I had to honestly look at what I had done to contribute to my own oppression, repression, suppression and depression. This was excruciating. To admit that I had contributed in any way to my own condition was agonizing. Believe me, I wanted to blame everyone around me for what they did, and they did do a lot of crazy shit, didn't they? But there came a day of reckoning in each of my abusive relationships and situations in which I had to say to myself, *What in the hell am I doing here? Is this as good as it gets?*

After I told my mother about the abuse, I kept waiting for her to rescue me, to protect me. To make my life better. When she allowed george to move back in the house, I waited for her to ask me how I was doing. I longed for her to take me in her arms and shelter me from harm. I was sure she would guard me and kick him out again after I found him in my room, masturbating over my bed. But he stayed. Surely it wasn't too much for me to expect that she would not want to be in a relationship with him ever again after I found him concealed in my closet like a lion watching its prey, stalking me and masturbating while I was asleep, when I was nineteen years old.

I kept waiting and waiting for her to say that the lips that violated my innocent vagina would never again touch hers, but they did. She longed for this man, and I sat by and witnessed it all. When I was a child, there was not much that I could do to change my situation, but as a grown woman, my life was mine to live. But I didn't think that I had an escape from the choices that my mother made. I was afraid to stay and afraid to leave. My mother launched a reconciliation effort with george when I was in college. The thought of his moving into the home again after all of this madness was unbearable and caused me to have a serious emotional breakdown when I was twenty-one. By then I was old enough to move out on my own—but I didn't. I didn't think that I could. I thought that was my life, as good as it gets.

I allowed my mother to continue to victimize me and put me in harm's way through her refusal to sever her relationship with george over the years. She works with him, laughs and talks with him, daily. I live next door to her now. She has him come to her house to fix things, though I have told her how painful it is to constantly see this man. She casually brings him up in our conversations even though I have told her that I get sick to my stomach when she wants to talk to him or about him. I didn't think I had an escape from my relationship with her; after all, she's my mother. I have to be in a relationship with her, I thought: this is as good as it gets.

When Duane was cruel and abusive emotionally, spiritually and physically to me throughout our marriage, I continued to stay because I had resigned to live a painful existence. I believe that was as good as I deserved and as good as it would get.

I have left it up to everyone except myself to determine how good my life gets. But actually it is up to me: I determine how good it gets by the things that I allow and don't allow in my life, by the people—no matter who the hell they are—I allow or don't allow in my life. God has honored my right to choose life or death in eternity; surely I have the right to choose life or death on this earth. So when I look around at my life and ask what the hell am I doing here? I now have no one to address that question to but myself. People have done some brutal things to me and around me, but I have the ultimate responsibility for how I live now.

I'll be the first to admit that when it comes to life, I got a raw deal. I had inexcusable parents, I had a hideous childhood, and I helped to create the breeding grounds for a heartbreaking marriage because that was as good as I thought it could get. Now, once I got free from all the crazy shit of others, guess what I was left to deal with? That's right, my own crazy shit. I found that my own shit is the most difficult of all shit to deal with. But if I really wanted to live, I was going to have to deal with it.

No matter what happens in our life, God has put inside of each of us a spirit of resiliency. I have seen people bounce back from, and excel, after experiences that I cannot imagine enduring, even as bad as my life was. It is not easy, but it is possible. God expects this of us, and I had to expect it of myself.

I had the choice of life or death before me. I kept waiting for others to choose it, but I had to choose it for myself and I had to choose it for my children, who are too vulnerable to choose it for themselves right now. As my children, they must deal with the consequences of, and the residuals from, my choices of life or death.

I have stayed way too long in way too many places because deep within, I settled. I thought this was as good as it would get for me. I decided to want less, and less is what I got. Less was enough for me. My visions, hopes, and dreams all shrank to fit into the small box of containment I had built for myself. I desired less, I expected less, I became less. I kept myself in a place where I did not belong.

My life was a roll of undeveloped film. Locked and protected within the container of film was the impression God made upon my soul when his mind first created me. Those images have been imprinted, but they have to be exposed in the right conditions to be fully developed, or they will be lost.

When my son was a toddler, he threw rolls of undeveloped film into the toilet. This is what we do with our lives when we expose ourselves to conditions that erase the imprinted images that God has impressed upon our souls.

I thought my life was as good as it gets because I thought I was as good as I deserved. When you don't think much of yourself, you can't expect much for your life. I thought that I deserved a fucked-up life because I believed that I was fucked-up. The truth is that I put all of my energy into maintaining the type of life that I felt I deserved. I wanted drama. I couldn't admit it then, but I can admit it now. I went wide-eyed into marriage with Duane, knowing that I had a fixer-upper. He had treated me badly when we were dating. Granted, it did get much worse after we were married. I may have dreamed of something better, even longed for something better, but I did not think that I deserved better than what I got. I did not position myself in relationships to do better or in situations to have better.

I wanted God to open the door for me, but I hadn't even approached the threshold. The Bible tells us that God will prosper what we put our hands to. I sat back and expected him to fulfill his word and prosper me, yet I hadn't yet touched anything. I sat on my hands with my thumbs up my ass and allowed my life to pass before my eyes, while I did little or nothing to make it better. That is, until I began this journey. Oh, and I can't stop now. I have come too far!

There is a change going on deep within me. I feel it stirring inside my soul. As I begin to nurture the desire for better, I gain the strength to see myself through the lens God views me. I get more and more restless, unsettled, and rebellious in and against the life I lived for so many years. I realize that my life is not working for me anymore. I no longer understand how I've lived, where I've lived, and even why I've lived as I have. The place inside that has made me feel small, invisible, and unworthy is slowly losing the immense power it once seemed to have over me, because I have cut off its energy source.

The place where the Spirit of God dwells within me has been too small and cramped. I'm giving it more room. I am slowly becoming willing to assume my God-ordained position in this world. I believe that I am here for a purpose, that my existence makes a difference. I once believed that I existed only to satisfy the salacious needs of others. I now believe that the reason for my existence is to help alleviate the pain of others who are living as I have lived, a life suffocated by lack, shame, and fear.

My old life does not fit anymore. I am being challenged on every side. It is difficult to endure, but the pain is purposeful. I do believe it is the pressing of the Spirit to let me know not only that change is in order, but my life depends on it. I am like the caterpillar struggling to burst out of its cocoon after a long deep sleep, transforming from the ugly, rejected creature that can only crawl, into the beautiful, adored butterfly that can fly freely allowing the whole world to take in her beauty.

One force within me is trying its best to coerce every fiber of my being to remain the same, do the same, love the same and live the same. Yet there is another pulling on my being to change, be different, do different, live different. A war is being waged for my very soul.

I can feel a desperate angst inside of me, something deep within begging and pleading for its life. It's terrified. It knows that if I begin to walk in the truth of who God created me to be, it will die.

I look closer, wanting to know who it is. Is it the voice of my abuser telling me that I am damaged goods, unworthy, good enough only to satisfy his degenerate desires under the cover of darkness? Surely it must be. Is it my mother who looked the other way, ignoring the signs that I was dying a slow, painful death when I was in the grasp of her husband? I know: it must be my ex-husband, who treated me like I was nothing and continued the abuse that was so horribly but comfortingly familiar to me.

No, it's not them. I cautiously move in to take a closer look, and I see that it's me. Oh my god, it's me!

The old me that was never me at all is clutching at my ankles, attempting to drag me out of my purpose. She is keeping me back from all that I would be, all that I could be, all that I am supposed to be.

I look up and I see a vision of my truest self walking on the path of my destiny. I can't believe my eyes, I am dazzling in all of my glory. I look back down and see the scared, damaged, shameful me, and she is holding on and she won't let go. She knows that her time is up, but she won't let go. I want to peel her hands off my ankle and finish the job, but I can't. My heart is filled with pity for her; she has been through so much. I can't just kill her. I don't want to become like all of the others who have abused her. I want to hold her in my arms and comfort her.

"Put her out of her misery," I hear. "Put her out of her misery. The only way that you can live is for her to die. You both cannot exist at the same time." It's the voice of God. I have been trying to coexist with my false self, and it's not working. For every step that I take forward, she takes five steps back. I have been pitying her, but she is out to kill me softly and slowly—the one that I've wanted to protect, she really isn't me at all. I now know that I must kill her if I'm to have any chance at all of living. It is either her or me. She was created from a place of depravity. To remain alive, she needs to feast on pain, suffering and destruction. She lives only if I die, and I live if she dies.

God has been building up my capacity to expect more out of my life. I realize now that I had limited him. He wants to do a new thing in me, but I've wanted to hold on to the same old things, like a toddler with a dirty, tattered security blanket. I was limiting God's work in my life by my own limitations. If I choose to believe that this is as good as it gets, and if that's all that I

133

open up my mind, heart, and spirit to receive, then that is as good as it gets. God is not going to force life on me; it is a gift for me to live if I so desire. And I do.

I don't consider myself completely freed from depression; I would rather say that I am no longer dominated by it. It is a formidable foe that I think will always be nearby, lurking in the dark shadows of my life. I keep it at bay by living an authentic life, the life that God intends me to live.

Every time I stop listening to my godly center, depression grabs my attention and forces me to take a closer look at how I am living. With every endeavor I make to go to the next level in life, like writing this book or leaving familiar places—such as my old job, in order to pursue teaching and inspirational speaking—a part of the old me dies. My false self would rather stay the same. She fights against the Spirit that desires to fulfill my purpose and destiny.

Depression rears its ugly head when I re-engage in unhealthy relationships, not just with men but also with family and friends. I catch a glimpse of it when I stop engaging in activities that bring life. I hear it tiptoeing around when I am not spending loving, quality time with my kids or when I am not taking time to refresh my soul.

The difference for me now is that I am not a victim of depression. I use it as a barometer and catalyst. When the alarm of depression begins to go off, I wake up and re-evaluate how I am presently living. I then determine what I either need to add to or subtract from my life. My false self, bless her heart, still fights for her life. I have to give the girl some props; she is determined to make it. She is like the pink Energizer bunny on steroids; she keeps going and going. Sometimes it feels easier to give in than to fight against my own self. But like I said, it is her or me. One of us has got to die. I choose her!

There were many days I would lie in bed with the covers over my head, sure that depression would be the end of me. But I have reconstructed and redefined the very thing that I thought would surely kill me. I use it to live, I mean really live my life, so that my life truly becomes as good as it can get.

Chapter Thirteen
Back to the Future

I cannot breathe. I literally cannot breathe. I try to speak, but I am unable to utter a single word. My mother is right next to my bed; I can't even turn around to face her and plead for her aid. In an abyss of private pain, I have people all around me, but I can't reach out for their help. This moment seemed to last for a lifetime, typifying the nature of my life: alone in pain, alone.

Although all I need to do is raise my arm a few inches so that I can reach the nurse call button, I feel as if I have to climb Mt. Kilimanjaro in order to do so. Somehow I manage to muster the strength to push it.

I am in the third stage of labor. Women have told me stories about this, but nothing they said could have prepared me for this experience. My baby's head is crowning—at least that's what the nurse told me. What it feels like is another story...it feels like I'm about to pass a blue-ribbon-sized watermelon through my ass.

I am in the labor room. I know my mother is here. I don't know who else is in the room. A nurse? A doctor? A friend? All I know is no one can help me.

Time has arrived for me to push, my heart stirs with a bit of excitement and a bit of fear. Is this treacherous journey almost over? Am I having a boy or a girl? Why is this baby's head so doggone big? Will I be able to make it on my own with two children? How long will I have to push? Can I have more drugs? Why did Michael Jackson turn white? I push as hard as I can. Not only doesn't the watermelon budge, it feels as if it has grown to "Ripley's-Believe-It-or-Not" size.

Tears roll down my face as I push. I cry tears of joy. I was glad that my mom was at my side. I still needed a mom and she was the only one that I had, good, bad and otherwise. I cry tears of sorrow that my husband was not. I cry because my beloved grandmother would never see the face of my baby, never rock it or sing to it the songs that her mother sang to her and she sang to my mother and to me.

"Push!" the nurse tells me. I push out the pain not just of my husband's absence from the room but of the anticipation of his future absence from my child's life.

"Push!" I bare down and push as if my life depended on it. As I push to bring forth life, I also bring forth death.

"Push! I push out the ache of rejection from my dad not being in my life.

"Push!" I push out the despair of being sexually abused by my mother's husband.

"Push!" I push out the agony of being emotionally abandoned by my mother.

"Push!" I push out the misery of my husband's every painful word and deed.

"Push!" I push out the disillusionment of unfulfilled dreams, hopes, and aspirations. "Push!"

I try to push again. I'm too exhausted. I need to rest. The journey I'm on is immense, for as I give birth to my son Christian, I am also giving birth to myself.

I don't know how I've made it through my life. I feel that I have died a thousand deaths. Still, I am here. Still, I am here. So many times I have asked God, Why? Why has there been so much pain in my life? What is the reason for my life? I have felt so consumed by all I have endured that there has seemed to be little left. When I looked back, all I saw was pain. When I looked at my present, all I could feel was pain. What is ahead of me? Can my life get better? Will the pain cease?

There was no escape from the pain that I suffered as a child. There was no place for me to go; there was no one to go to. The only escape I found was in my own mind.

Still, I packed my pain within my soul tighter than sardines sealed in their own juice in a can. I have forgotten more about my childhood than I am able to remember. In my forgetting I have lost some of the good memories. But I had to forget. I had to forget even as it was happening. It was too much. It was more than I could take; it was more than I could bear.

I stopped crying. I think I was afraid to cry. I think I was told not to cry. I think I forgot how to cry. I stopped crying.

Honestly, as bad as things were, I still had no idea of the depth of pain that was inside me. We all lived as if nothing was happening, as if everything was fine and dandy on the home front. No matter how difficult it was to make it through the night, by the morning I had to be in character and ready to act my part, to convince the world around me of what it wanted to believe: *"All is well, don't worry; you don't have to do anything to help me, I need no help. Go on and live your life. I'm fine. I'm fine. Please don't allow my pain to keep you from enjoying yourself."* It didn't. Everyone's life around me went on as usual, while the pressure of my reality intensified inside me.

Have you ever seen a volcano erupt on a nature show on television? Pressure that has been building up for years causes lava to burst out of the top of a mountain and pour through the sides. The birth of my children opened up my life and caused all that was buried deep with my soul to erupt with great force. I began bulging at the seams of the soul. They opened me up. There was an explosion of great proportions that neither I nor those around me were prepared to contend with. Much like the people of Pompeii, we were all caught off guard when the volcano erupted, and no one escaped.

There have been many times, more than I can count, that I wished myself dead. The only way I believed that I could escape the tragedy I called my life was death. To some that might sound like the hard way out. Honey, let me tell you something: when you are in the funky armpit of total and absolute despair, death can look pretty damn good. Sure, I was afraid to die, but I was more afraid of continuing to live my life as it was.

I had hoped that george would just stop what he was doing to me. I hoped that my tears would make him stop. I hoped the wrongness of his actions would make him stop. I hoped that something inside of him would make him stop. Instead of stopping, the abuse intensified. There came a time, then, when I stopped believing that the pain in my life would stop. I had given up all hope.

I would cry myself to sleep at night. I felt excruciatingly alone. I had to escape my life, but I didn't know how or where to go that would be safe for me. I eventually accepted this was my life and I was going to have to either learn to endure it or just curl up and die. I decided to live a life of masquerades. I taught myself how to be present in body but absent in spirit. I sealed off my emotions and went deep within myself. I built a wall around my heart to protect me from further harm, or so I thought.

Ahhhhhhh! This numbness was just what I needed. For the first time in a long time, I could not feel the pain. Oh my God! It felt so damned good not to feel the pain. I had been in pain for so long, I had forgotten what it felt like not to hurt. The absence of pain felt so good that I did not see what was happening inside of me and around me. I was too busy enjoying the lack of pain. I was numb. I wished I had thought of this earlier; it would have saved me a lot of grief.

I used to love to play with my friends; I now stayed closed up in the house while my friends played outside without me. I would play alone for hours with my Barbie dolls in my perfect pretend world. I mean, I played with Barbie dolls into my high school years. I couldn't bear to part with them. (I still have some Barbie dolls packed away in my basement, and every now and then I take my time and stroll down the Barbie aisle at Target, with or without my daughter.) It was too painful to feel all my friends could see the shame that was on my soul. So I kept to myself. It felt better. It felt worse.

Drawing was another escape for me. I believe I was in second grade when I really began to draw. I borrowed a drawing instruction book from school, and I wore the ink off the pages from reading that book over and over and over. It opened up a brand-new world for me to escape into. I could create the world the way I wanted it to be when I drew. The characters that I drew became my friends. Like my beloved Barbie dolls, they didn't judge me, they didn't shun me. They accepted me just as I was, and I needed them.

⁂

In every way possible, my kids literally saved my life. I guess they were my new Barbie dolls, in a way. Even though they have loved me for myself, just as I am, they inspired me to want to be better, to live better, to be my best self. I wanted to be that for them. I wasn't sure if it was possible, but they made me willing to try and try again.

Even after my children were born, there were still extremely intense times—when I was going through another depressive episode or things were really bad between Duane and me—when I would once again be consumed with thoughts of killing myself. Now, though, I would not allow the desire to ease my own pain to override my determination not to cause my babies the pain and devastation of having a parent commit suicide. For their sake, I couldn't do it; for their sake, I wouldn't do it.

I chose to live, but inside, I was still dead. I knew that I could not settle for living my life like that, or I might as well go ahead and finish the job. I made up my mind that if I was going to live, I was going to live.

Having made that decision, I discovered that deciding to live had been the most difficult and the most powerful step. After that, life actually got a little bit easier. Not easy, but easier.

Now, that I had made up my mind to live, I mean really live, I had to start letting go of all of the elements of my life that were killing me. I was not prepared for what the decision to live was really going to cost me. Life can be had, but it ain't cheap.

After the birth of my first child, Alexandra, —Who would be surprised considering my life history?—I had a severe bout with post-partum depression. I was ready for the insane asylum. I was just days away from checking myself into the psych ward. Actually, I was a few days past needing to do it. It took every bit of strength and faith that I thought I had, and every bit that I thought I didn't have, just to make it through every minute of every day.

No one around me knew how far gone I was. They never did. I was such an accomplished actor that I played a convincing role as a sane and happy new mother. Inside, I was out of my cotton-picking mind! Don't get me wrong here, I did love and adore my beautiful new daughter, and I was beyond happy to be her mother, yet tormenting psychotic thoughts of harming my precious baby constantly bombarded me. While nursing my beautiful baby at my breast, I had to block out images of throwing her up against my bedroom wall. While singing to her the sweet lullaby that I made up just for her; I wrestled with thoughts of putting a pillow over her head and suffocating the life out of her little body. Every moment that I was awake, I was plagued by thoughts so intense, and so dreadful it seemed my mind would rupture.

You are probably asking yourself the very question that I asked myself again and again, until I finally got an answer. How does a woman who is happier than anything to be a mother of such a luscious daughter, go from tenderly nursing her baby at her breast to contemplating infanticide?

Here's what I discovered. Remember that I told you, in order to survive I had to cut off pain from my life. If, as a child in the midst of abuse, I had continued to feel the full impact of my pain, I would never have survived. So I could not feel pain. That's a good thing, right? Well, let's take a closer look at the results . . .

My intoxicatingly beautiful daughter mesmerized me. She was all that I had ever wanted in a daughter. She was lovely as a tulip-covered field with a rainbow of butterflies hovering over it; she was sweet as cotton candy at the county fair on a hot summer's day. I wanted to love her with a love that I had never known. She began the process.

Christian continued it. After the birth of Christian, my son, my handsome little son, I wanted to be able to shower him with love. I saw both of my kids as the greatest gifts that God ever gave me. They were precious, and beautiful, and funny, especially Christian.

When they were babies, I showered them with hugs and kisses. When they got older and wanted to return those kisses and hugs, it made me feel like I was out of control. It used to hurt me for my kids to touch me. I felt that I was dirty and if they touched me they were defiled, too. I would shun their touch. What I wanted and what I needed was to be able to feel them. I couldn't, no matter how hard I tried; I just could not feel them.

I went deep inside myself to excavate the capacity to love my babies with a love that they deserved. What I discovered was that when I tried to access the place in my heart where a mother's love grows, to open up the floodgates I ran head first into a rock-solid wall. Remember, this was the wall I had built to protect myself.

The thing was, pain wasn't the only emotion that I turned off. When I turned off pain, I turned off pleasure. I had numbed the pain, but I could no longer feel the love either. I was so anxious and excited to love my kids without reserve that I turned the feel-o-meter way up. I didn't realize that when I unleashed love, I was also unleashing the years of repressed anger, pain, loneliness, anxiety, fear, confusion, depression, and unforgiveness that had long been packed away and sealed. When my feelings came back, they came back with a vengeance.

I hate going to the dentist. I mean I really, really hate going to the dentist. My only saving grace when I just can't put off an appointment another year is the happy gas and the Novocain. The Novocain makes me not feel the pain, and the happy gas makes me not care if I do—I stop caring about where I am or about what is being done to me. The dentist can poke, prod, and drill, and I couldn't care less. I sit there with my eyes closed, high as a kite in the sky on a breezy afternoon and loving it.

For some silly reason, every time I go to the dentist, I seem to forget what comes after my mouth begins to wake up again. I go out of my way to drink hot coffee or tea to wake my mouth up, because I hate the residual numb feeling. Then my mouth wakes up—and I ask myself, Now why in the world did you hurry up that process? You should have just enjoyed the absence of pain a little while longer. When my mouth awakens, I feel every poke, prod, and drill of the dentist's earlier work. Literally, I feel it as if it were happening right then.

Alexandra—and subsequently Christian—caused me to want to free myself from numbness. I wanted to hurry up and wake up my heart to feel again. I wanted to feel love and to give love. I wanted to know intimacy without pain. I had to reawaken.

But first, I had to go back and feel what I had avoided feeling. All of the unfelt emotions were all lined up, waiting. After all of these years, they were all still waiting for their turn to be felt. They were all there, they hadn't gone anywhere, waiting, just waiting in me, binding me up deep inside my soul. Alexandra and Christian woke me up from the state of the living dead in which I had become resigned to reside.

It's hard to describe, but it is as if I woke up from a deep, deep sleep. It was like the Michael Jackson video "Thriller." I felt like one of those dead folks walking and dancing around the street!

Upon awakening, I could not believe what I saw. As I began to look around, I saw that my life had been out of control for a very long time. After Alexandra was born and I had become pregnant with Christian, I decided that I would not and could not, continue to live as I had been. It was then that I came to the agonizing, but honest, epiphany that my marriage to Duane was an extension of my abusive childhood. I realized that I could not stay married to him and live. Leaving Duane was my renaissance. When I became willing to let go of him to save my own life, it opened up a floodgate for all of the bullshit to exit out of my life.

It allowed me to come to another realization that was well overdue: I could not continue in the relationship with my mother and her ex-husband as it had been. For the first time I would have to come face to face with my mother and honestly tell her of my utter disillusionment with her as a mother. I had to tell her of the devastating consequences I had suffered because of the selfish, ill-directed, insane choices she had made. All this time, I had been laughing and smiling with her as if we had the best mother-daughter relationship in the world. We didn't. As much as I loved her, I hated her for what she had done to me, and I needed to express that to her.

I was going to have to go back and deal with all the things that I had buried away and thought were forgotten. This was one of the most difficult legs of my journey, because it was going to shatter the masquerade into a million tiny pieces. The jig was up.

I set up a meeting with my mother and asked Alex to help mediate it. In this meeting, I confronted her about her failure to protect me from george. I told her the pain and anguish that her decision to stay with him had caused me and I demanded to know why she made the choices that she did.

I wish I could tell you that she had all the appropriate responses that a mother should have so that in the end we embraced and pledged our undying love for one another, but that would make this book fiction, and it's not. She was in deep denial and could barely force out a half-assed apology for her actions. She was extremely defensive and full of sorry excuses. I had burst the bubble of her fake little "all is fine" world. My confrontation of her prodded her to take the look at herself that she wasn't willing to take. How dare I challenge her image of perfect mother and perfect family? She acted like I was the one in the wrong. She sat there and cried like I had offended her. I realized at that point she was too entrenched in denial to be able to respond to my pain.

Hey, sometimes you win, sometimes you lose. Sure, I had wanted much more than I got from my mother in that meeting. But it turned out that she didn't have anything to give me. I had wanted her to restore me, but that wasn't her job to do.

Disappointed and longing for more, I still left the meeting feeling empowered. I was so proud of myself for finally having the courage to open my mouth and voice to her the things she had done over the years that scarred my soul. I felt better, the way you do after a satisfying bowel movement following days of constipation.

The next thing I did was set up a meeting with my mother and george, again with Alex serving as the mediator. This meeting was a lot more difficult than I thought that it would be, but in the end it proved more fruitful for me than the one with my mother alone. You should have seen her. It was pitiful really. She was so happy that she was not in the "hot seat" this time. She told george that he had to sit there and take it just as she had had to.

Being able for the first time to speak of the vile sexual things that george had done to me was freeing, despite his denials. I had let those dirty little secrets stay just between him and me, and they were festering. Voicing them severed the dark tie that had still bound us to each other. I told both george and my mother that I was done with "playing family." I told george that he would no longer be a part of my life in any way. I told him that he would not be a part of my children's lives in any way. I wasn't pretending anymore.

Something else happened that night that I had not expected, could not have even begun to anticipate. When I gave voice to those dark, unspoken secrets, there was a transfer of shame. I had felt ashamed of myself all those years for the things he did to me, but that night, after I spoke them out and left the meeting, the deepest level of the shame I had been living under and according to was gone. It had been george's and my mother's all along; I had mistakenly thought it was mine.

I mean, I shit all over them! Not my shit—oh no, no! It was their shit. It was their funky-smelling, life-stealing, worth-destroying, child-sexing, body-violating, girl-prostituting, trust-breaking, fake-ass-acting, secret-carrying, child-neglecting, heart-breaking, dream-shattering shit that I had been carrying around in my soul all those years. Now it was transferred from me to its rightful owners, geoge and my mother. Hallelujah!

I had finally done something that I hadn't thought I could do. I gained the strength to cut off the sick relationships and end the façade of the perfect family. I finally let down the curtains and exited the stage.

As hard as I had tried, I found that I could not go forward in my life until I went back. I had tried for so long to repress and ignore my past. I thought that there was freedom in ignoring and not dealing with it; but I was only giving myself a false sense of security. I had to go back and feel the pain, or I could not feel the love that I so desired to give and receive. I had thought that the secrets, shame, and shit were dead and buried and could do me no more harm, but they did. They seeped into every aspect of my life. They showed up on every job and in every relationship, like a deadly poison that has been released in the air. Every time I endeavored to be more, they were there to give me surety that I count not.

I went back to my past so that I could love my babies and receive their love. I went back to my past so that I could deal with everything that was keeping me from being the glorious woman God had created me to be. I went back so that I could face every lie I had believed about myself and cast it down with the truth. I went back to reclaim the innocence that was stolen from me from the people that I loved and trusted the most. I went back to redeem a frightened little six-year-old girl who had been left behind, to wipe away her silent tears and embrace her. I went back to tell her that she was safe now. I went back to pull her out of the ominous shadows of disgrace and shame. I went back to rescue her, and she didn't even ask me why it took so long. I went back to save my (inner) baby and in so doing, I set myself free.

Chapter Fourteen
Forget you!

Dear george,

After years and years of being a part of the living dead, enduring depression, low self-esteem, isolation, loneliness and despair, medicating myself with work, school, food, sex, or shopping, crying myself to sleep, or crying myself awake during nightmares starring you,

I've decided to receive God's gift. A gift that will benefit you indirectly . . .

That gift is forgiveness.

Now, please don't get me wrong . . .

I am not weak.

You are not strong.

I was not mistaken—you know every vile thing that you did to me!

However, I have decided to live my life—fully! Entirely! Joyfully and freely!

And in order to do that, I must let go of dead weight, namely, you.

Now, let me educate you . . .

Forgiveness is not for the frail.

This is not to be confused with a license to ever think of hurting me again.

This is not an invitation for restarting a relationship with me. You had your chance to be a father to me; you instead chose to misuse and abuse me. Too little, too late. Sorry!

Forgiveness is a way of freeing my soul by holding my Father's hand while looking you dead in the eye to say: You're forgiven.

Now, let me help you . . .

Being forgiven doesn't mean that you're excused.

It means that you're so inexcusable that you could never say the right thing to justify your wrong.

So why should I sit here and wait for something that you're incapable of doing and I am incapable of receiving . . . from you.

And to show how insignificant you now are in my life, I release you . . .

I free you . . .

You no longer exist in my world.

Forgiveness means that I no longer focus on you—I forgot you!

In fact, saying "I forgive you" is really like saying, "Fuck you!"

I say this in the nicest way that I possibly can.

I mean, fuck you in the sense that what you did to me no longer matters,

It's no longer important to me, my life, my hopes, or my dreams. I no longer give it the power to define me.

So when you see me, please, don't pity me.

I want you to know that I have truly freed you when I say . . .

Fuck you!

Fuck your mama for bringing your sorry ass into the world.

Fuck your fucking daddy who failed to teach you how to be a man.

Fuck your perverted soul that caused you to lust after an innocent six-year-old girl, your own stepdaughter, who loved you as a father.

Fuck you, you mother—and—daughter-fucking asshole.

Fuck your demented mind that allowed you to bring harm to a harmless soul.

Fuck the money that you offered me to do you "sexual favors."

Fuck your fucking twenty-dollar bill that tried to prostitute me.

Fuck you for hurting me rather than protecting me.

Fuck your illiterate uneducated ass that thought I was only worth twenty dollars.

Fuck your coward ass that never got help or counseling.

Fuck your stupid ass that thought I would ever want you to be a grandfather to my kids.

Fuck you and your Polaroid camera that took pictures of my naked innocent body, you pedophile son-of-a-bitch!

Fuck the lie of thinking I'd want you to give me away at my wedding.

Fuck you for playing the proud father at my wedding.

Fuck the shit, shame, and secrets I endured to protect your nasty ass.

Fuck the fake image of our "perfect family."

Fuck your nice-guy image to the community when you were really a child-fucking pervert.

Fuck Mississippi for letting you out of it.

Fuck Wisconsin for letting you in.

While I'm at it . . .

Fuck you Sam Payton for not being there to protect me.

Fuck you Duane for all of the crazy-ass shit you put me through; for not being the husband or father that your kids and I needed you to be.

And fuck anyone else that I needed to but failed to mention.

I forgive you all!

My, my, my! I feel so much better now!

I didn't realize that forgiveness was so good for the soul. I am so glad I did this!

Sincerely, Lilada

P.S. When I have the time, I want to write you another forgiveness letter entitled "Kiss My Black Ass!"

I have a secret that no one would suspect about me. I am a nice, kind, churchgoing woman. I am respectful, respectable, fun-loving, and funny. People enjoy being with me. Heck, if I didn't know better, I myself would not suspect this secret: underneath it all, I am an unforgiving person. In my mind, unforgiving people are nothing like me: they have a humped back, warted nose and hands, and a permanent evil expression etched into their face. I have my issues, but certainly I am not an unforgiving person! No way, not me!

I mean, if you had hurt me I'd forgive you, sort of, but you could bank on the fact that I wasn't about to forget what you've done to me. And you could be sure that I wouldn't let you forget either. I would hold on to the offense, and if you hurt me again, you were going to get "the list." "The list" was my recital of everything that you had ever done to hurt me. My painful memories consumed me.

I didn't realize that the old grudges I was holding on to were taking up valuable space that I needed for new beginnings, new love, new peace, and new definitions of myself. I was holding on to the old me—the way those people, places, and things made me feel about myself. By being unforgiving, I was stunting my own growth, stunting my relationships, hindering my ability to raise my children to be healthy, because I wasn't. I needed new lenses, new internal filters through which I could clearly and correctly view my self and the world around me.

When I was a new homeowner, I didn't know that I was supposed to change the furnace filter regularly. I lived in my house for about three years without changing the thing. All the air we breathed for those three years went through the same filter. No wonder we kept getting colds. When we don't change the filter through which we receive life, we keep recycling the same old shit—this hinders us from being able to move forward.

As I held on to old issues, old wounds, old injuries, old insults, old disappointments, old painful experiences, they become the filters through which I lived and experienced my daily life. I magnified their power and increased the strength of their impact upon me. I mistakenly believed that holding on to the pain, the sorrow, the times and ways my trust had been betrayed kept the wrongdoer captive. What I discovered was that there was indeed a prisoner, but that prisoner was me.

I felt justified in my stance. I had been wronged, and I was not going to let the offending party forget it. Why? One reason was the pain of being hurt. Subconsciously I felt that if I did not forget, nor let them forget, it would protect me from being hurt again. It didn't. It just caused another set of painful experiences and painful residuals.

I learned that I cannot make others see the pain that they caused me through my eyes. Sometimes they just won't get it. Sometimes they don't care to get it. Sometimes they don't even remember the things that I have allowed to continue to hold me captive. Sometimes they have moved on with their own lives and just don't give a damn.

I have had a secret desire to go back and rewrite my past, to change all of those who have hurt me and brought me tremendous pain into the nice, lovable people my heart desired them to be. When they could not or would not become such lovable people, more resentment and more unforgiveness would build up in my heart, starting the cycle anew.

There is nothing I can do to make my mother the mother that I had always believed she was, the mother that the world believed I had, the mother that she thought she was. I can't go back and change the fact that she sacrificed my ass to save her face. I cannot go back and undo the fact that she put me in harm's way and left me there to fend for myself. I can't change the fact that she still has a relationship with the man who brutally defiled my body and my soul. Those are the choices that she made, and she has to live with them.

When I would talk to my mother and she could not or would not recognize her emotional abuse and neglect of me, I would be re-offended. When she could not or would not see that it was outrageous that she still worked with george, laughed and talked with him, had him come to her house to fix things, as if what happened to me was no big deal to either of them, I was re-injured. I

149

would feel like the little girl again, who was thrown to the wolves by her own mother. Wounded.

Part of me wanted to punish her and never allow her to escape the pain that she caused me and the mistakes she made with me. I created a box for her, and I would not let her get out. My whole life was horrifying, and it was all my mother's fault.

Now surely she is—was—to blame for a lot in the past. Past is the key word. I am a grown woman now with children of my own to raise. Harboring resentments against my mother was allowing the past to keep me locked into a victim mentality. I was creating present-day pain for myself by holding on to the past. Not only had I put my mother in a box, but I had created one for myself.

Nothing that george could ever do or say could erase the devastation he caused in my life. So every time I saw george—at my mother's house, on the street as I was driving to work or church, at the neighborhood gas station—I was re-abused. I could not see him without seeing myself as a little girl and the disgraceful things he did to me. I would have flashbacks of his performing oral sex on me or ejaculating on me, or the feel of his rough hands on my body. How could I forgive what was still occurring in my mind? I felt as if he had stolen the best parts of me, the parts that could not be redeemed. I constantly felt like the abused six-year-old girl.

When I had to fight in court and argue outside of court to get Duane to pay child support, when he petitioned the court for me to pay him alimony, when he went for years without paying child support or seeing his kids, I was re-offended. His lack of fathering our kids seemed to be a direct attack on their worth and mine. I felt like the abused, worthless wife, even after we were divorced.

When I could not forgive my father for not being in my life as I was growing up, every time I attended a family event and felt like a bastard child when my aunts, uncles, cousins, and even my own sister did not know who I was, I was re-discarded. I felt like the little girl who was not good enough for even her own dad to love her.

When someone steps on your foot and asks your forgiveness, you are glad to oblige. Now say that same person keeps stepping on that same foot, again and again and again. It gets harder and harder to forgive. After a while, forgiving is impossible because the offense continues. It's not until you can bring an end to the offense that both forgiveness and healing can begin.

I think part of my need to hold on had to do with a belief that those who had wronged me still held essential pieces of the puzzle of my worth, of my life, my existence. Somehow I felt that unless they redeemed the situation—begged my forgiveness and pledged that if they could do it all over again they would do it differently, thus redeeming me in the way I wanted to be redeemed—I could not be whole. Now that is giving crazy-acting folks and crazy situations too much power!

As I allowed—and I say "allowed" because I was fighting and kicking throughout most of my journey toward forgiveness—God to work on my heart with forgiveness, I began to see that I was my own problem. My allowing these people to keep "stepping on my foot" had been locking me into a perpetual cycle of victimization, persecution, oppression, and shame. I had given them power to define me, my worth. I had given them power to define my past, my present, and my future. I had to forgive them to set myself free.

Knowing that I needed to forgive didn't make it any easier to do. I still hated the idea of forgiveness. I know for a good Christian, that is a horrible thing to say. It is horrible, but it is also true! Why should they get away with what they have done to me? I will be justified! I will be vindicated!

Unforgiveness. I have heard many times that it is not about those who need forgiveness, it is really about the forgiver. Yeah, I would think, but they get away scot free and I am left with the scars. Somehow that did not at all seem fair.

I have come to the realization that I have spent far too much of my life playing judge, jury, and prison guard to those who have hurt me. The truth is, there is nothing any of them could say or do to eradicate the wrongs and make them right. Why not get on with my life and stop expecting something that could never happen? So I had to forgive. I didn't know how it was going to go, but I had to do it.

Lilada Gee

I started with my mother. I had tried to forgive her many times but had failed, because every time I would talk to her about her actions, choices, and decisions, she was defensive, in denial, and insincere. She has never been able to fully understand my feelings about it all. She has never taken full responsibility for her wrongdoing, because she either cannot see or refuses to see the depth of it. I had been looking for a certain intensity of regret that she has not been able to give. This time was a bit different. We sat down and talked over a meal, and something amazing happened during our conversation about the past. For the first time I realized—I mean I really seized the truth of the fact—that the ridiculous, damaging choices my mother made had nothing to do with what she thought I was worth. They were about what she thought she was worth. It was all about her, not about me at all. She was wrestling with her own demons, and I had gotten caught in the crossfire. My mother didn't know her own worth; how could she be the one to determine mine?

As I cried over my waffles, I looked at my mother. She looked so small, almost like a little girl who, as a sixty-four-year-old grandmother, still wondered what she was worth to her own mother. She sat there and cried about the wounds that were still open from her relationship with her mother and the choices her mother had made. She didn't have anything to offer me.

She gave me a blessing that day: she told me how much she loved me and how much she wished for me to live a life that was wonderful, full of purpose, passion, and love, despite the past. I could not fully receive the words she said, because her actions have never been consistent with her words. Still, I felt a release that was not of my mother's or my own doing. The strength of God came into me, empowering me to forgive my mother, really forgive her. I could let go. I could let go of the anger, the resentment, the hate. I could go on with my life and no longer live under the shroud of insignificance. I had taken away the key I had given to my mother to unlock my soul. I literally felt a great heaviness lifted off my body, mind and soul. It felt remarkable.

I decided, Hey, maybe this forgiveness shit isn't as bad as I thought. So I went on to my second mission—the next person on my "hit list," my ex-husband, Duane. I still had a number of transgressions to forgive him for. While forgiving him, I also needed to ask for forgiveness. I called him up and started the conversation by telling him that I was sorry for the pain our divorce had caused him. I knew that I could no longer be married to him, but my leaving was not an act against him but an act for me and for the kids. I apologized for the pain that my unresolved residual issues from sexual abuse had caused him during our marriage. I told him that I did not want to continue to argue and be angry, that I hoped we could move forward in peace for the sake of our children.

By the time the conversation was over, I was crying so hard I could hardly talk. I told Duane that I forgave him for all the unnecessary drama, abuse and overall dysfunction. I also forgave him for not being a father—a real father—to his children. When Duane left me with the full emotional, spiritual, and financial responsibility of raising our kids, it had broken me down. I felt more betrayed by that than I did by our marriage mania. It was one of my worst nightmares coming true: my kids growing up without their father, like I did. I wanted so much more for them. I felt that his neglect reflected what he thought they were worth, and that had opened my own wounds even further.

I came to the understanding that Duane's treatment of me during our marriage and his failure to father our children had less to do with me and them than it did with him and whatever he was dealing within his own tortured soul.

The pain that Duane caused me was because of the pain that he was in, not because of my worth. I couldn't continue to be angry with Duane for making me feel that I was worthless, when that's how I already felt before I even knew that he existed.

As for myself, I really desired to move on in life and in love. But I knew if I tried to take all the negative emotions that I still harbored toward Duane into a new relationship, it would destroy that relationship like a raging flood. It would be over before it even had the chance to begin. In order to move on, I knew that I would have to let go of all of the resentment, bitterness, disappointment, frustration and regret. There was no detour road that I could take. If I truly desired to move, I would have to travel this leg of my journey. So, I forgave him, and I moved on.

Now the next step was a doozy! I knew that I still had areas in my heart of unforgiveness against george. I felt them holding me hostage; and I longed to be free. My plan was to write him a letter to tell him that I forgave him. Writing would be easier than facing him, I thought, but it would still do the job. As you have read, the letter was written. It felt damn good to my soul to release so much of the anger and resentment that was trapped deep within, but...

One day I was on my way home, and there he was on the corner. I looked the other way, as I would usually do, and kept driving. As I continued down the street, a voice in my spirit said, *"Stop. Do it now."*

I said you're kidding, right? You want me to do it, right now?

"If not now, when?"

As much as I wanted to fight against the spirit within, I knew that this was the time and the place. I didn't want to go a moment longer in the state that I was in, so I turned my car around and I went face to face with my foe. I called george over to the car. He looked scraggly. Unshaven, teeth missing. I thought to myself, is that what I have allowed to imprison me all of these years?

He looked a little scared as he approached my car. I hadn't spoken to him in years, other than telling him to stop speaking to me. He probably wondered if I was going to go postal on his ass. Instead, I told him that I forgave him.

You could have knocked him and me over with a feather. We both heard the words, but neither one of us could believe that I was saying them. I meant it, I could hardly believe it myself, but I really and truly meant it. I have to admit, I did have to catch a glance of myself in the rearview mirror during the middle of the conversation, to reassure myself that it was in fact me talking. He asked if this meant that he could speak to me now; he offered to buy me lunch.

I told him, *"Whoa Nellie! Let's take this one step at a time. There is nothing you need to do in order to earn my forgiveness. I give it freely."*

So has my mother changed? No, I don't think so. Almost thirty years after I revealed to her the truth, she still works with him and doesn't see why that should change; he's still welcomed at her house. I've told her how it all makes me feel, but things are still the same. Yet, I chose to love her, albeit from a safe distance. Has george changed? Who knows, I didn't stick around long enough to find out. Are we all family now? Hell no! But that's not what forgiveness is about.

Forgiveness isn't about changing others; it's about changing yourself and making your life fertile for growth. Those who have offended me may never change, but the precious lesson that I learned was that I didn't have to wait for them to change in order for me to change.

How about Duane? Has he changed? Is he a totally different person? Well, our relationship has definitely improved since I made a decision to forgive him and acknowledge my wrongdoings in the marriage. In fact, I must admit that Duane is beginning to feel less like a foe and more like family. We can have civil conversations now where absolutely no profanity is exchanged. Of course, this doesn't mean we agree on everything; and it sure doesn't mean that he doesn't occasionally neglect child support payments, or visiting with the kids. As a matter of fact, as I write this he is unemployed, once again. And once again, I have to carry the full financial brunt of taking care of the kids. I have been there, and done that.

Rather than getting a J-O-B to enable him to pay child support, Duane has asked me to cut things out of my budget that will impact the kid's quality of life. All the while, he and his wife aren't sparing any expenses on their lifestyle. They are living in a brand-new house, driving a brand-new SUV, and living the good life. Don't get me wrong, I understand that if he prospers, so do my children. However, I don't feel it is acceptable for him to live high on the hog, enjoying all of those wonderful things, while not financially supporting the kids, not to mention neglecting to pay me the thousands and thousands of dollars that he still owes me for the years he didn't pay child support.

Having said all that, things are still so much better than they have been in many years. The peace that we are establishing between each other is not just a blessing for us; but much more for our children. Last summer Duane provided airline tickets for the kids to spend some time with he and his wife. I traveled with them to the visit. We all went out to dinner and later Duane and his wife invited me to stay with them overnight. All of us sat down together in their living room watching a movie. I would have never foreseen this in a million years! I silently laughed to God and asked, *"Who would have thought it?"*

Ooo-wee! Let me tell you something. I felt clean inside. I felt like the weight of the world had been lifted off my soul. I began to look different to myself when I looked in the mirror. I looked like a dark film had been lifted off me. I saw a spark that I hadn't seen in my eyes since I was four years old. Others began to tell me that I looked different, prettier, happier, younger. They wanted to know if I was using a new skin regime. Honey, what was going on in me could not be bought for any amount of money. I had lifted the final veil of shame off my own self by giving others my forgiveness. Through the venue of forgiveness, God was undoing in me what had been done. No wonder God forgives us seventy times seven times a day, this feels good!

There are many ways one can achieve forgiveness. Each individual must follow the path that is laid before them. Sometimes the one who offended us may be dead or otherwise unavailable to talk to. Writing out our forgiveness can be a very therapeutic experience. Sometimes you just have to say, to your offender, "Fuck-you;" in other words, "You no longer have any control over who I am or will be," and move on in life and LIVE!

Chapter Fifteen
9 1 1

I put my car in park. I take a deep breath, and hesitant as I turn off the ignition. I don't want to go inside, I silently say to myself. Tears begin to well up in the corners of my eyes, but I fight them off. I sit in my car as long as I can.

I look at the clock and see that I am now running late. I slide out of my seat and reluctantly step outside the vehicle. I know that I have a very long walk ahead of me.

I try to keep a positive mental attitude—be strong!- even though I want to weep like a baby. As I approach the doorway, my steps seem to go into slow motion. As a reflex action of shame, I glance over my shoulder to see if anyone I know is seeing me walk through the doorway, over which there is a sign in large black letters: PSYCHIATRY DEPARTMENT.

I make a point of giving the receptionist a smile, even though it's forced, as I tell her I am here for my eleven-o'clock appointment. I try to act as if I don't really need to be there, as if I'm different from the rest, but I am not. I am in deep need of emotional healing.

I have gone about as far as I can on my own. I have done a lot of really difficult work on myself. I have seen a great deal of growth, but I need some help to get better, to be whole.

I have so many internal stigmas to work through as I take my seat and wait to be called by my doctor. I must be crazy if I need to go to a counselor. I can't be a real Christian if I can't pray myself out of depression. And let's not forget the shame. I should be able to do better all by myself. Admitting that I need professional help is admitting that I am weak, frail, broken. But the truth is, I am. I really, really am.

I decided to start seeing a counselor when I was eight months pregnant with Christian. I'd had severe post-partum depression with Alexandra, and Duane and I were together then. I was sure that I was going to get it more intensely now that we were separated and on our way to a divorce. My stress level had really increased as I struggled to embrace the reality that I was about to become a single mother of two children under the age of two.

A few months earlier, I preached a message entitled "Do Something Different." Yes, I was still preaching despite all the internal hell I was going through! Hey, if God can talk through an ass, surely he could use me, right? I could preach and mean it; but I was still wedged between a rock and a hard place. Nevertheless, I encouraged my listeners to evaluate their lives and honestly determine what they needed to do to make some major changes.

Why does my own life feel so difficult right now? Why it is so hard for me to make the changes that I so deeply desire to make? I keep feeling stuck, afraid, ill equipped. I am in the wrong place at the wrong time. I can't be who I am, I can't be where I am. I start, I make some progress, then I stop again. I start, I make some progress, then I stop again. I start, I make some progress, then I stop, again.

I am defeating myself with the actions I take and with the actions I don't take. What do I absolutely need to change in my life to change my life? What do I need? What do I need to rid myself of? I don't know where to begin. Where do you begin changes when your entire life no longer fits and there is no other life available to live? Is it my job, my weight, where I live that I need to change? Do I need a man? Yeah, that's it, I need a man!

Do I need to de-clutter my life of people, places, and things that weigh me down? Is it the unresolved issues, underlying anger, my relationship with my mother? Is it all of these things, or is it something I have yet to consider? All of this thinking makes my head hurt. I don't know what to do, but I do know that something must be done! I need a breakthrough. I just don't want to be unhappy anymore.

Those are some of the many questions, rantings, and ravings that come out in my sessions with Dr. Brigham, my counselor. She listens, she asks questions, and she listens some more. Sometimes I feel better when I leave. I've reached a breakthrough that will help me move a little bit further along my journey. Sometimes I feel worse. Something I have said, something she has asked, has struck a deep wound that I didn't realize was there and I have to take a few steps back to be able to take a few more steps forward.

The counseling helps. Dr. Brigham confirms the diagnosis that I already knew, but she diagnoses another condition I hadn't known about. I have post-traumatic stress disorder. Like a Vietnam vet, I have been reliving the atrocities of the war of my emotionally violent and abusive childhood. The second diagnosis is what I am surprised by. She tells me that I have an anxiety disorder. Dr. Brigham eases into suggesting that I consider taking an anti-anxiety drug. "No, thank you!" is what I tell her. *"Hell no!"* is what I think. Coming to a counselor is already more than I could bear. Taking a brain-altering drug is out of the question.

I continue to refuse what Dr. Brigham is sure would be a help to me. *"Can we try some other things first?"* I anxiously ask. So we do. We do the talk therapy thing, and it helps some. We do the behavior modification thing. I wear a rubber band around my wrist. Whenever I have a self-defeating or negative thought, I pop myself as hard as I can with the rubber band and say, Stop! That helps some too, but none of it is enough to bring about the changes that I desperately want to see happen.

I want to love my kids freely. Instead, I look at them through a plastic bubble, unable to fully feel my emotions toward them or allow them to feel theirs toward me. I am hurt. Unhappy.

Anxious. Always fearful. Bitchy. I go days, weeks, and months without a good night's sleep. My energy is low and my hope is even lower.

Confusion. Frustration. Aggravation. Helplessness. Hopelessness. These are the overwhelming emotions I am feeling. I feel let down and disappointed in myself and in others. I have felt this way for far longer that I should. I want to feel better. Oh God, I want to feel better. I can't go on like this. Thoughts of suicide roll in my mind. I already feel like I am dead—what's the difference?

Pictures of Alexandra and Christian flash before my eyes as I consider ways I might kill myself without too much pain or too much drama. Pills. Yes, pills will do the job. Nice and slow. No blood for anyone to clean up. I will just fall asleep and never wake up again to this painful world. Then I see images of my kids again, and I imagine their lives without me. Children of parents who have committed suicide must carry deep pain and shame for the rest of their lives. I can't do it! As much as I hurt, I can't end my own suffering to begin the suffering of my children.

I had been having anxiety attacks and depression episodes since I was a child—obsessive worrying, negative "what if" questions, scary thoughts, irritability, insomnia. All this time, I thought that I was just a worrier, that I was stressed out by the pressures of college life, being in an unhappy marriage, being a single parent, being in this situation or that situation. I thought I was just bitchy and fearful. I didn't realize that these feelings and behaviors were really not me at all.

Dr. Brigham told me that these were all symptoms of a classic case of a generalized anxiety disorder. Part of me was relieved to at least have a name to give my problem. Another part of me feared that I was under a lifelong sentence, that the impact of the sexual abuse in my childhood would haunt me forever, infiltrating my feelings, attitudes, moods, behavior, relationships, jobs, parenting—my entire self. How unfair! How cruel! I have done a lot of work on my issues to become a better person, especially a better mom, yet I am stuck with a diagnosis that I cannot will away.

I began going to therapy more frequently; I read countless books and articles on anxiety. I know I can beat this thing! *"Just try the medication,"* Dr. Brigham would encourage me. No, I can't! I surfed the web, tried positive mental attitude, self-talk, affirmation techniques. I tried all of the natural remedies I could get my hands on, such as flaxseed oil, gotu kola, valerian. I tried relaxation techniques, deep breathing, and massage therapy. I tried pleading and begging God for mercy and deliverance.

I tried some of these by themselves and some in concert with others. Some helped a little, some helped a lot, but none of them cured my basic maladjustment, anxiety. I was still in great emotional distress and inner turmoil. I had come to the end of my rope. I had to tie a knot at the end so that I could hold on. Medication was that knot.

Even after I had given in and decided to try it, I still felt a bit ashamed. I feared that I would be losing control of myself, even though on a cognitive level I knew I shouldn't feel ashamed any more than a diabetic who needs insulin or a cancer patient who needs chemotherapy.

You should have seen the drama with which I took the first pill. I mean I was dramatic even for me. I was petrified that the medication would turn me into a mindless zombie. I brought the pill to my mouth with a trembling hand. I put it in my mouth and slowly gulped it down. As I swallowed, the little white pill felt like it was the size of a football. It got stuck in my throat halfway down.

I wish that I could say, poof!, like magic, all my problems instantaneously disappeared. It didn't work exactly like that. But things really did get better.

The medication made it easier to deal with my life. It took the edge off. I was calmer, less irritable, and my thoughts calmed down. I continued in therapy, and it was more effective. I felt as if I now had a bit more of the upper hand. It took awhile for my body to adjust. Initially my dosage was too strong and made me sleep a lot. My doctor adjusted it, and my body adapted.

161

Lilada Gee

At first, I felt as if God had turned a deaf ear to my numerous desperate pleas for a miraculous deliverance. I still believe that God could have miraculously healed me, but I learned several important lessons through the process. First, I realized that I had been doing the same things but expecting different results. That, they say, is one definition of insanity. Second, it was important for me to fight for myself. This helped to challenge my victim mentality. As a victim, I have tended to feel that I have had no control over what happens to me. When I began to put up a struggle, a fight against the things that held me captive, I felt stronger, I felt empowered.

There is no shame in needing help. The only shame is having help available and refusing to take advantage of it. I learned from this experience and decision that if old coping techniques aren't working, it is important to try out new forms of help that are offered. The first or second new solution that you try may not be the right thing. It may not work out the way you had hoped, but it's better than just doing the same things. Sometimes it's most important to move—no matter what direction you go, just move!

Two years later, I am still taking Celexa for anxiety. I had hoped to be off it by now, but I'm not. I am taking only half the dosage that I started with, so that's good.

What's important is that I am stronger than I was. I am no longer a victim. Now when I come up against an overwhelming situation, I may rest for a while between rounds, but when the bell rings, I get up and fight like my life depends on it; because it does.

Chapter Sixteen
A Woman of Worth

I am A Woman of Worth!
Adapted from The Message Isaiah 60

Get out of bed, Lilada!
Wake up. Put your face in the sunlight.
My bright glory has risen for you.
I have risen in you; My sunrise glory breaks over you.

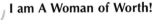

Nations will come to your light, kings and queens to
your sunburst brightness. Look up! Look around!
Watch as they gather, watch as they approach you.

What's that we see in the distance? Its ships from the
distant islands, loaded with riches, with silver and
gold, and backed by the name of your God, the Holy
One of Israel, showering you, Lilada, with splendor.

Foreigners will rebuild your walls, and their kings will
assist you in worship. Your gates will always be open—
day and night, receiving deliveries of wealth from all
nations, and their kings will be your delivery boys!

Not long ago you were despised, refused, out-of-the-
way, unvisited, ignored, and you thought you were

unworthy. But now, Lilada, I have put you on your feet,
towering and grandeur forever; you are a joy to look at!

Lilada, I, God, am your Savior, your Redeemer, Champion! I'll give you
only the best—no more hand-me-downs! Gold instead of bronze, silver instead of iron,
bronze instead of wood, iron instead of stones.

I'll install Peace to run your life. There'll be no more stories of abuse in your land,
no more robberies, no more vandalism of your soul.

Lilada, I will be your eternal light; I, your God, will bathe you in splendor.
Your sun will never go down; your moon will never fade. I will be your eternal light.

Lilada, your days of grieving are over!
I am your Father-God. At the right time I'll make it happen!

Swoosh! All of a sudden and without warning, the protective sac of fluid that has been the only home this little life has known bursts and gushes out from around her. Automatic contractions of her mother's body begin to insistently coax her out of the womb. She has no choice but to respond. To not respond means certain death. To respond means traveling into the unknown. Which is worse? Which is more frightening?

The birth process is an arduous journey for a baby. They must leave behind the comfort of all that they have ever known, in order to receive more than they could ever imagine. An instinctive knowing tells her that it is time to start the journey. Though she has become snug and comfortable in the womb, there is a pulling of all of life's forces around and within. Our spiritual rebirths are much the same as a natural birth. I use the plural, rebirths, because as we live, we must go through several rebirth experiences.

I had become comfortable in the womb of my life. I was comfortable with the sights, sounds, and smells of the familiar. Then all of a sudden and without warning, the life I had been living gushed out from around me. Life's forces told me it was time to make a change. I, unlike the child being born, had a choice regarding how to respond. Yet, not to respond still meant sudden death. The harder the contractions became, the more my world was trying to tell me that it was time to make that journey. This has been my journey.

Worthless. A feeling of worthlessness permeated my entire being. Though no one ever looked me directly in my face and told me I did not matter, the culmination of the events of my young life communicated that message to me loud and clear over and over and over again. I walked around feeling as if I should apologize for my existence. I believed I was a disappointment to all those around me, especially God. I felt that I was not what I should be; I definitely was not what I wanted to be, but I believed I was all that I could be, and what I was wasn't good enough.

So what was I worth? Five minutes of wicked pleasure and ejaculation into a filthy rag? Ten dollars? Twenty dollars? Was that his best offer? How about my mother—what was I worth to her? The mortgage payment? The ability to afford a second family car? Saving face with people who didn't give a damn anyway? What was I worth?

For me, the lack of worth was non-negotiable. There was no way that anyone, even God himself, was going to convince me otherwise. I passionately embraced the certainty that I was worthless. I was thoroughly convinced that I did not have value, never did, and never would! I thought there was no possibility that things would ever change. Just when I was snug and secure living my false life, God showed up and decided to turn my whole world upside down and right side up.

Jesus said, *"As a man thinks in his heart, so is he."* In my opinion, this is one of the most powerful statements in the Bible. Deep within my heart, I thought that I was of no value. How I decided to see myself, and it was my decision, though I had a lot of help in forming my invalid assessment; impacted every thing in my life. It affected every life experience I had, every decision that I made, every relationship that I was involved in and how I loved and parented my children. All of these were and are determined by who I think I am. How I view myself makes the difference in whether I decide to curl up and die or live my life.

Much of my torment came from my allowing everything and everybody but God to identify me. As I surrendered myself to a false identity, I allowed it to determine who I thought I was. I fought desperately to maintain that identity. You can clearly see from my story that I continued to surround myself with people, places, and things that kept me in the prison that once was imposed but others, but later was self-imposed.

I surrendered my soul, body and mind to the emotional, verbal, physical and sexual abuse of my mother, of my husband and of george. I held on to it all for dear life, despite the hurt and humiliation, because it had become comfortable and familiar. It was all that I knew and was accustomed to; then it became all that I sought.

I desperately looked to my mother to define me and give me worth. It took me a lifetime to discover that since she didn't know who the hell she was and what she was worth, she couldn't tell me. I looked to george to define me, thinking that he could give me the worth that my father didn't. In his perversion, he took advantage of my love and trust and he ravaged my soul to satisfy his own. Now even more desperate and in need of worth, I turned to Duane to fulfill me. I believed that all I needed was a good man by my side. I was so sure that my husband was going to be the one to redeem me. He couldn't help me, he needed redemption himself. I felt that they had all let me down and had destroyed my life.

It was easy for me to continue to blame them all for how I was living. But the truth was to make a radical and lasting change in my life, I had to accept the fact that I had played an active role in my own captivity. One of my most painful revelations of truth was that I had continued to allow my abusive and devastating experiences and those who abused me, to determine my identity and dominate my life. I had been pointing the finger at everyone for all the shit that was in my life, but me. Oh yes, Verline, george and Duane did dump a lot of shit on me, but it was I who permitted it to remain in and rule my life.

Truth? It is easier said than believed. To begin my quest for truth, I had to go back to the one who created me. I had to be reminded that I was created in the image and likeness of God. I had to be reminded that God never forgot who he created me and always intended me to be. God's definition of me had to take authority over what others had done to me and hadn't done for me. I had to learn that no people I had known or had been associated with, no places I had been or life experiences I had endured and no things that had been done to me or I had done, could eradicate God's intentional purpose for my life and his ever abiding love for me.

God waited for me to decide that I had had enough of shit, mine and everyone else's, in my life. When I did, I gave him the space to be God in me. He lovingly stepped in and gave me a makeover more radical than any we have seen on a talk show. God even outdid Oprah.

I had to face some life-changing questions that were not easy to answer. I had to ask myself, am I willing to relinquish the old to embrace the new? Am I willing to make the necessary changes to detach myself from the people, places, and things that maintained the old, tired, damaged and counterfeit version of myself and seek out the people, places, and things that could help me build a firm foundation of the new, exciting, abundant and true? I had to determine if I was willing to let go, even if the new were not the ones from whom I most desired redemption. This was my defining moment. When my eyes were opened to the truth, would I respond?

By myself I could not make the life changes I frantically desired. But neither could God bring about those changes without my willingness and active involvement in the process. I wanted to see a miraculous move of God in my life, but I wasn't always willing to do my part of the work. I prayed to God to just do it in my sleep. *"When I wake up, let it all just be done!"* That would have been nice, but the fact was, I had to do the work. He promised to give me the strength, but I had to use it to move from where I was to where I was created to be.

No part of this journey has been easy, but God has been with me every step of the way, loving me and encouraging me. He helped me to draw the people into my life who would support the God-dentity instead of the I-dentity, absentee-father-dentity, abusive-stepfather-dentity, neglectful-mother-dentity , the abusive-husband-dentity, that I, with the help of others, had created. It is not the I, or the he or the she, but the God who lives inside of me that determines who I am!

As long as I tried to ascertain my worth according to the value system of the world around me, I could never measure up. As I began to allow myself to be defined by God's word, I found that my true worth is and has always been based in him. Nothing I had ever experienced could change who he predestined that I was to be. As I developed my relationship with my Father-God, I no longer lived as a bastard who did not know her father. God acknowledged me as his own, and he legitimized me, and gave meaning and value to my existence.

I had to relinquish the assumption that I did not have worth because of my past and begin to ask God how he wanted to use me because of my past. There is a reason for each experience I have had. Nothing goes to waste. I am so glad that God and his purpose for my life are bigger than my own thoughts and limitations. Despite myself, God was determined to show me that I am his own.

My command now is to live according to God's divine purpose for me. When I focused on my painful past, disappointments, and difficulties I was totally missing what God was doing. I hated my life and wanted to trade it in for a better model, one that was unblemished. I assumed that the hopes, dreams, and aspirations in my heart were only cruel reminders of what I could never achieve because of my past. The reality was that because of my past, I could.

If we will allow it, God will redeem our pain. His Word tells us that by the whips and cuts on Jesus' back, we are healed. Just as God took the pain and brokenness of Christ and empowered and redeemed it for healing for our sake, so will he take our pain and suffering and redeem it. He will use it as a powerful instrument for the healing and blessing of others. God will use everything that you have believed was a curse upon your life to bless others.

Perhaps when we are going through pain, it is not the enemy who is in control of it after all. Perhaps God in his infinite wisdom knows which experiences we each need to endure to make us into the person he designed us to be. Perhaps the womb is just the first place in which God shapes us. He uses our life and the experiences and relationships we encounter, both good and bad, to continue the process of forming us into his image. If we learn to not fight the process but rather yield to it; and in every experience anticipate the divine redemption God will bring to it; we will find that we are no longer victims, but victorious.

I have experienced God's grace, mercy, and healing firsthand. I can offer God's grace, mercy, and healing to others. If I had not gone through those wrenched life experiences, I would not have the powerful deliverance testimony that I now have. Would I want to relive my past? Hell to the no! However, I am no longer consumed with bitterness about it, because I can now see the purpose in it. I now seek to find who I can help, who I can encourage, who I can inspire to live a better life than they are currently living.

I have learned that it really is not about what we go through but how we go through. There are those I know who have gone through experiences similar to mine, and were completely devoured by the suffering. Many who have endured what I have gone through (and less!) have committed suicide or decided to throw their lives away to drugs and alcohol or destroy the lives of others because of their own pain. It really boils down to how we react to what we experience. Think of a family with two children, who encounter virtually the same experiences—say with an alcoholic father and an abusive mother. One becomes a drug addict, the other a successful doctor. They had the same mother and father, lived in the same house, so why two different outcomes? The one realized that they still had a choice in the life that they could live, despite it all. The other did not.

I used to see my life story as a curse. I now see it as a blessing. I intend to use the individual and collective experiences of my life for God's glory. Things that I used to be ashamed to whisper, I now boldly proclaim in a pulpit over a microphone. The wondrous thing is that I see God working healing in other women because of my pain.

I want my life to mean something. The only redemption for my life is for my suffering not to have been in vain. If I can help a girl, a woman, a mother, a daughter escape from her internal prison, then I think I have fulfilled my purpose. It would be much easier to keep all of my horrific, shameful secrets to myself. But I tell it and I tell it all so that I can free someone else. No tear that I have cried is in vain! If I had not endured my life, I would not have the power of God to heal the pain of others. I now praise God for my life, all of it! And even now, when trouble rises, I look for God in each experience-and I always find him!

Thank you for going on this journey with me. It has been quite the ride, hasn't it? I told you things aren't always as they seem. Women ask me all the time, "How did you heal? Grow? Change?" Most, I think, want a nice, sweet little religious answer. There was nothing nice, sweet or easy about this journey. I cried. I cussed. I fussed. I had to be willing to lose everything; and I did, to gain more than I could even imagine. There were many times I wanted to give up and give in. I was sure I was going to lose my very mind, and a few times I think I actually did. I was willing to give up my life, and in that surrender, I truly found it.

The writing of this book has cost me my life. What I mean by this is that I have lost the ability to continue with the life I was living before I began this process. I can no longer hide behind façades; I can no longer be comfortable with mediocrity. I can no longer pick and choose the truths of God that I will embody and adhere to, because this book has challenged me to remove the veil of insufficiency that I hid behind for far too many years. The one to whom much is given, much is required. I have been given much truth. I am now required to embrace and live my life according to that truth.

This journey didn't make me worthy. What I found out on this journey was that I was worthy all along. I was just like Dorothy and all the gang in The Wizard of Oz. I already had the thing that I so very deeply sought. I was already worthy, because God made me that way and he never changed his mind about me.

I feel like a brand-new baby!
I have my whole new life in front of me to live, love and enjoy!
I am fabulous! Blameless! Shameless! Wonderful! Loving! Lovable! Beautiful!
I was gloriously made! I am joyful! I am enjoyable! I bring laughter!
I bring light! I bring delight! I am a song of joy!
I am whole! I am free. I am the apple of God's eye.
I am a woman of worth!

Chapter Seventeen
Can You Still Live How You Are Living?

You've read my story, so now let me ask you about yours. What mess have you gone through that you believe you cannot get the funk off of your soul? What life defeating experiences have you been exposed to in your past which are still impacting your life in so many destructive ways today?

Can you still continue to live how you've been living?

Are you tired of all of the same shit in your life—yours and everyone else's? What is the result of staying the same? Is it worth it? When you live a crazy-ass life, you are never the only one who is affected. So even if you can stay the same, can your kids continue to live how you've been living? If you are married, can your spouse continue to live how you've been living?

Can you still continue to live how you've been living?

Right now, at this very moment, you can decide to make a change in your life. You no longer have to live your life according to pain, fear, depression, unforgiveness or needless destructive drama. With one step, you can make a decision that will change your life for the better for an eternity. For those of you who know God, its time for you to live the better life, the abundant life that he has provided. Now you know better, do better. Change is not only possible, it's necessary.

For those of you, who don't know him, it's time to get to know your Father, God. Through everything that I have gone through in my life, God has been the constant. You may be asking, "huh, if you went though all of that with God in your life, why do I need him? Honey, I can do bad all by myself." The thing is, if I hadn't gone through what I endured, you wouldn't be reading this book right now. I wouldn't be able to tell you that I have been there and have gone through that; so I know you can live better than you are living. I went through some horrible experiences, but it was all with the purpose of proclaiming, with power and purpose, that you don't have to anymore.

Like my story, Jesus endured pain and suffering in his life all with a purpose. His purpose was to bridge the gap so that mankind could be reunited with our Heavenly Father, who truly desires to be in relationship with his children.

If you are tired of how you've been living, Jesus said "Come unto me and I will give you rest." Not in the sweet by and by, you can have peace today in your mind, your heart and in your soul. It may seem impossible to make the changes that you truly desire in your life, but you can! With God all things are possible!

The Prayer of Salvation

Dear Father God,

I am tired of the way that I have been living my life. I realize that I have not been living a lifestyle according to your plan for me. I bring to you all of the things that I have done to others, and others have done to me. I bring to you all of my hurts, pains, angers and disappointments. I bring to you all of my hopes and my dreams, and I ask that in return, you transform me into the person that you created me to be. I ask that you restore every broken place in my life. I want to fulfill the purpose that you have for me. I want to use everything that I have gone through in my life to help others live better. Please forgive me for the things that I have done wrong and help me to forgive those who have wronged me. Live in my heart and give me the strength and desire to live for you. Amen.

Chapter Eighteen
What in Hell Made Me Write This Book?

Writing this book is one of the most difficult things I have ever done. In the process, old memories have been stirred up that I would much rather have left forgotten. When I was a child I would often close my eyes and pretend that I was somewhere else so that I could not feel the pain of my present existence. I would dream of beautiful places and things that did not exist in my real world. At the time, that was what I needed to help give me the strength to make it through. I think I would have been totally consumed with the pain otherwise. Like those around me, I turned my face away from the pain that I endured and looked the other way.

As I wrote, the grief often overwhelmed me. Some days when I was writing, I had to stop; and even after stopping, I was still consumed with raw emotion. I cried, I screamed, I cussed. I was angry. I was sad. I was scared. I felt alone. I felt disarmed. I felt stripped of everything I had ever used to protect myself. What I was seeing in the memories of my mind and feeling in the memories of my soul was terrifying, but it was the true, uncut version of my life.

I hated what I was seeing and thought I could not bear what it made me feel. I had to face every dark and scary place of my life. I wanted to turn and run away, to get away from everyone and everything. Then I realized that wherever I ran, there I would be. To make my reality better, to pursue the abundant life Christ sacrificed to give, to mother my children with my body, mind and spirit, to embrace my worth that had seemed always just out of my reach; I had to go on this journey.

When I was a teenager, I once proclaimed, *"I want to pull people out of hell."* A few months ago, I was attending a women's event. I went to the altar for prayer. There God gave me a beautiful and powerful vision that would fulfill not only my prophecy but, much more, my destiny.

All over the world, there are women like you who are living in hell day by day because they do not know who they are or whose they are. In the vision, God showed me once again that I would pull women out of their hellish lives into his freedom and liberty. You are why I write this book.

I pray that you are one of those women. I pray that the words of this book reach up from the pages, grab you by the heart, and free you from the secrets, shame, and shit that you have been carrying around for far too long. You've come this far, please don't stop now! I encourage you to dare to continue your own journey through prayer and counsel. You're worth it—go on this journey! My sister, I wish you traveling mercies.

I have listed a few resources to help get you started on your journey. I hope some of my favorite reads and websites will be a source of information, strength and encouragement to you.

Books

The Bible — Two of my favorite versions of the Bible are The Amplified and The Message. Of course the entire Bible is a great resource, but if I tell you to read the whole thing it may feel overwhelming. Below I have listed some of my favorite books of the Bible that I would recommend you read:

Psalms — a beautiful collection of poetry and songs, the book of Psalms is such a lovely way to learn about the characteristics of God. I love it!

Matthew, Mark, Luke and John — want to know what Jesus would do? These four books give a great picture of Jesus; how he lived and loved those around him.

Proverbs — this book of wisdom gives advice on good old common sense living. That brother Solomon had it going on!

II Timothy — this book really encourages godly living.

Hebrews — This book helps to clarify our faith. Chapter 11 is all that!

Galatians, Ephesians and Philippians — I love all three of these books. They are short, but powerful. They are passionate letters written to new Christians to encourage them to live in the freedom that Christ died to give us all.

Genesis — I am a history buff, so I always enjoy reading Genesis. There are some great stories of trial, tribulation and triumph in this book.

The Book of Ruth — This is a great story about a woman who had her desperate life redeemed.

Jesus & the Hip Hop Prophets
My brother Alex Gee wrote this book with his friend John Teter. It takes a look at the music of

Lauryn Hill and Tupac, examining the spiritual message that they share with the world through their lyrics. A must read is the chapter that my brother wrote, Brenda Had A Baby....deep!

Simple Abundance

Sarah Ban Breathnach

I love this book. It has some great words of wisdom, and fun and insightful activities that help you to see how wonderful you are. One of the greatest lines from this book is "I am what I am and what I am is wonderful!

Yesterday I Cried

Iyanla Vanzant

This is a fantastic book. It takes you on Iyanla's journey from damnation to redemption. I was very inspired by this read.

Websites

Oprah.com — You know Oprah is the girl! Her website is awesome. There is a section on her site called Live Your Best Life. There are great tips, insights and inspiration to living a wonderful life. There is always something new on this site, so keep going back.

Paulawhite.org — Paula White is a powerful minister who has been through about everything you can imagine; yet, she has overcome. She has written some great books that you can check out on her site.

Bible.com — This site is so cool. You can read the Bible on line book by book or look up specific scriptures. It has a great search feature where you can just add in key words to find a scripture or to find scriptures on a particular subject. This is a great resource for someone who knows the Bible very well and for someone who has never read the Bible before.

Siawso.org — Surviors of Incest Anonymous. This site has support for survivors. This is a good place to find resources for healing. Be sure to check out their 12 Step proclaimation.

Batteredmothers.org — This site has a lot of helpful information for mothers who find themselves in abusive relationships.

Epilogue

Writing this book has helped heal so many untreated wounds in my life. One particular area of unresolved pain was my on-going tumultuous relationship with my mother. I am happy to say that some major things are changing; creating the space for us to work on developing a renewed relationship.

In fact, my mother is making efforts to hear my pain and to acknowledge the impact her actions (and non-actions) have had upon my life. She recently sent me an e-mail video of the song "Because of You" by Kelly Clarkson. In the e-mail she wrote "I accept responsibility".

I asked my mother to write a paragraph for my epilogue. This was her response:

"Some readers may be wondering how I feel regarding the release of my daughter's book "I Can't Live Like This Anymore!" Well, the first emotion I feel is pride. Secondly, I'd like to express my complete belief in the absolute unconditional love my daughter feels for me, as well as the complete and unconditional love and respect I have for my daughter. I don't feel ashamed—but I do feel unquenchable remorse because I failed my daughter as a mother—which subsequently changed the complete course of her life.

Love takes many paths, we do many things in the name of love and honor, but the truest sign of love is when you can say to the one you love, and have injured, I messed up, forgive me. "

Your story may not end this way. I encourage you to remember—with or without the acknowledgement and remorse of the one who has injured you—you still have the power to heal.

❦